MW00768765

Confessions

of a

Reluctant
Missionary

Chronicles of My First Mission Trip to Honduras

Confessions
of a
Reluctant
Missionary

Steve Norwood

Pleasant Word
PW A Division of WinePress Group

© 2010 by Steve Norwood. All rights reserved.

Cover design and photography by Steve Norwood.

Pleasant Word (a division of WinePress Publishing, PO Box 428, Enumclaw, WA 98022) functions only as book publisher. As such, the ultimate design, content, editorial accuracy, and views expressed or implied in this work are those of the author.

No part of this publication may be reproduced, stored in a retrieval system, or transmitted in any way by any means—electronic, mechanical, photocopy, recording, or otherwise—without the prior permission of the copyright holder, except as provided by USA copyright law.

Unless otherwise noted, all Scriptures are taken from the *Holy Bible, New International Version®, NIV®*. Copyright © 1973, 1978, 1984 by Biblica, Inc.™ Used by permission of Zondervan. All rights reserved worldwide. WWW. ZONDERVAN.COM

Scripture references marked KJV are taken from the *King James Version* of the Bible.

ISBN 13: 978-1-4141-1664-8
ISBN 10: 1-4141-1664-0
Library of Congress Catalog Card Number: 2009912512

I must no longer depend on pleasant impulses to bring me before the Lord. I must rather respond to principles I know to be right, whether I feel them to be enjoyable or not.

—Jim Elliot

To

Mark and Sharon Searcy

&

Reverend Israel Gonzalez and

Dr. Floripe Hernández de Gonzalez

Contents

Preface

MY GRANDPARENTS WERE missionaries in the Belgian Congo for thirty-six years. All three of their children were born there, including my mother, who was born soon after they arrived in 1915. English was not her first language—it was Tshiluba, the dialect of the region where they lived near the Congo River.[1]

After "Gramps" and "Granny" retired, we lived with them in Savannah, Georgia, while my dad was being operated on and treated for tuberculosis in Texas after World War II. He was not expected to live but eventually pulled through. Gramps was the pastor of Eastern Heights Presbyterian on East Thirty-seventh Street, in Savannah, and I heard much about his experiences in the Congo. He often preached on the topic of foreign missions, emphasizing his life verse, Mark 16:15—"Go ye into all the world, and preach the gospel to every creature" (KJV). He even based the title of a 16 mm film he produced on this verse—*Go Ye*. I had the verse memorized.

Yet I never felt called or really encouraged to become a missionary. In my teens the Congo was embroiled in a bloody revolt. Missionaries fled for their lives, yet Gramps at the age of 70 returned to work with United Nations relief until he too had to be evacuated. I went on to college and drifted into the field of education, lacking much direction, purpose, or counseling. Nevertheless, it's been a successful career and one I've enjoyed, but when the opportunity came following my retirement to taste the life of a missionary, I was intrigued. Having heard about the mission field all my life, I was curious to see what it was all about. But I did have some reservations—not about traveling but about whether the trip would be worth my time, trouble, and expense. *After all*, I thought, *I could be on the beach in the Virgin Islands*. So join me now on my trip to Honduras, where I was a reluctant missionary.

Chapter 1

One Good Reason

IT'S JUST A dirt road high in the mountains of central Honduras, but a cathedral in Rome couldn't be more beautiful, nor God closer. We're a group of about twenty tall, smiling, and light-skinned *Americanos*

who are handing out "Christmas shoe boxes"—actually plastic gift boxes—to children although it's the day after Valentine's Day. In Spanish these treasures are called *regalos*. Regardless of the season or language, all children love gifts. To these children with caramel skin, coffee eyes, and licorice hair, being presented with their own plastic box stuffed with goodies evokes reverence, awe, and wide-eyed wonder. Though they are eager, their happiness is hidden, their joy reserved and—perhaps like us—foreign. Most poke through their boxes, pulling out various toys and dolls to show and compare, but many hold the boxes to their chests unopened. Some must be shown how to remove the snap-on lids. Those choosing to wait gently peer inside or look up from the bottom just for a glimpse of what awaits them in the sanctity, if not privacy, of their own homes—likely a small, one-room adobe hut with a tin or tiled roof and dirt floor.

It's hard to believe that just a few months earlier I was indecisive about going to Honduras to help with the distribution of Christmas gift boxes for children. It

was then that I had begun to fill two "boxes" of my own—one with reasons why I *should* go and another with reasons why I *shouldn't*—go, that is. I kept waiting to hear the one good reason that would make my decision clear.

"When we first started doing this," says Mark Searcy, our mission leader from the United States, who looks over the flock of brown faces and squints in the afternoon sun, "most of the children didn't know these plastic boxes could be opened and didn't even know how. When they get home, the plastic boxes are valuable, too, and more practical than the traditional recycled shoe box. These can be used to store sugar, rice, or other food—they're rodent proof."

"But what'll we do with the big cardboard boxes?" I ask. "Take them back?"

"Nah, the parents will almost fight over them. We never have to carry any back. You'll see," he says with a wry grin beneath his floppy, olive-green canvas hat and close-cut mustache.

Midway between the Caribbean and the Pacific, small villages or *aldeas* perch on the sides of vaulting mountains in this coffee-growing country eight hundred miles north of the equator. These mountain hamlets offer no typical streets or stores. Homes are scattered and tiny. Schools may be nonexistent, meager, or miles away. Fledgling churches meet on the side of a road, in a clearing, or at someone's home until resources are pooled to build a humble place to worship. Their web of roads with no guardrails or pavement is as rugged as the surrounding pushed-up peaks—Gothic steeples crowned with ghostly mists and soaring eagles.

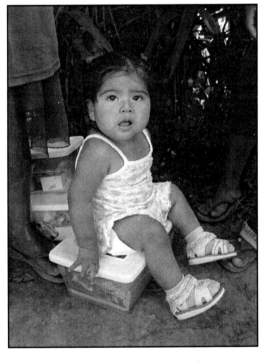

The route we take snakes up the soft, steep mountainside, passing though tropical vegetation, crops, and occasional clusters of crumbling mud homes and barefoot children. They run to see our caravan of five vehicles pass with noisy, groaning engines and churning tires in billows of dust. Large, stacked-high pasteboard boxes contain hundreds of plastic gift boxes. The children know that with the *Americanos* come "candee" and other good things.

With the help of the local pastor, word of our coming—the day, time, and location—has preceded us. Not only by word-of-mouth but by something one might not suspect, especially in an area where few have electricity or telephone lines. Yes, even here, a scattering of cell phones now help carry the drumbeat of news from *aldea* to *aldea*. And so the people come—in pairs and in small groups—women, babies, toddlers, school-aged children, and teens—all walking or being carried. Wearing flip-flops and walking the unpaved inclines carefully, they come down from higher up, and they come up from trails below.

Most men are working in the steep coffee orchards, but a few appear in the uniform of the typical Central American *campesino*—a common term describing the indigenous subsistence farmer or peasant. Carrying razor-sharp machetes, they wear wide-brimmed cowboy hats; loose-fitting, sweat-stained shirts; baggy trousers; and muddy rubber boots. As the crowd gathers, they stand to the rear, separate from the women, and watch curiously with crossed arms and faint smiles on weathered, unshaven faces. Women, wearing loose, ankle-length dresses, stand beside a stick-made fence of patched barbed wire and prickly bushes bordering the road. With soft, white cloths draping their shoulders, they cradle nursing babies and listen to the Bible story about the Prodigal Son, who ran out of money, friends, and food.

"Would you like to eat with *the pigs*?" the lady asks in Spanish to the throng of children who are standing in front and listening attentively to every word. Her lips are against the microphone, and the portable PA system squeals with feedback right on cue as she asks again, "¿Los cerdos?"

A boney, brown dog ambles with impunity around the hordes of legs, dirty feet, and sandals, sniffing the ground for a wayward morsel. The canine's less-interested twin takes a nap under the teacher's table beside a bewildered toddler, who has also found shelter from the masses and shade from the sun.

The children inch closer and their eyes grow wider at the teacher's question. "The pigs?"

"Noooo," they answer with a shudder, white teeth sparkling from innocent faces. Their clothes are clean but well worn and wrinkled. I see a variety of shorts, jeans, jumpers, and T-shirts—many with logos and slogans in English. Their clothes seem more typical for children back stateside but tell a story, too, I think. Missionaries have been here before.

We are in the *aldea* called Buena Vista, our vehicles parked randomly on the precarious roadside at the foot of a little knoll on a narrow razorback or cordillera. The mountain ranges in Honduras twist and turn, pushed up in zigzagging patterns from the squeezing and still active seismic pressure between the continental plates that run through Central America, a land of forty active volcanoes. A bumpy trail leads to the top of the little pinnacle surrounded by coffee plants. There in a clearing of hard clay rests a pile of volcanic rocks that were hand carried from the cliffs below—an altar of sorts. It's a small but significant start to where a church for Buena Vista will one day be built. It will have a nearly three-hundred-sixty-degree view of the valleys below—a variegated, green blanket laced with streams, patch-worked with crops, and hemmed in by distant greybeards—the gigantic mountains ranges of central Honduras.

Atop the rise, I look over this small, almost forgotten country. I marvel at the Eden-like rain forests in the distance that provide an undisturbed home to monkeys, jaguars, sloths, orchids, and toucans. Resting above these mountain empires I see, like a descended New Heaven, mysterious cloud forests swaddled under a pure, white canopy of perpetual mist, a holy shroud that hovers over the skyscraping peaks, the tallest measuring 9,416 feet in elevation—almost two miles high.[2]

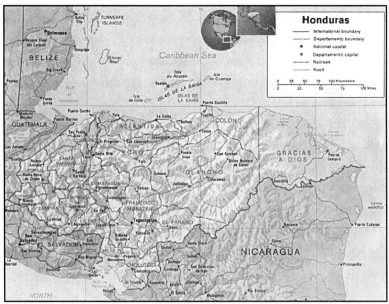

Honduras is one of seven small Central American countries clustered between Mexico and South America and is the third largest in area with forty-five thousand square miles—about the size of Ohio.[3] It is one of the poorest and least developed countries in Latin America. With a population of about 7.5 million, over 50% live below the poverty line.[4] The per capita gross national income is only $1700 ($4.65/day) with about one-third earning less that two dollars per day—the international poverty line.[5]

Near the narrow isthmus of Costa Rica and Panama, Honduras and Nicaragua form the second peninsula below Yucatán. It's the large land mass elbowing into the Caribbean that presented an obstacle to Christopher Columbus on his fourth and last voyage in 1502. He named the easternmost tip Cabo Gracias a Dios or "Cape Thank God" because the opposing headwinds and weather suddenly broke following a violent storm on his coastline trek. This event also gave Honduras its name, which means "depths" in Spanish. The complete phrase by Columbus is said to have been "Gracias a Dios hemos salido de esas honduras" or "Thank God we have come out from those depths." [6]

Chapter 2

Bendiga Señora—Dios le Ama

AFTER THE BIBLE lesson, Scripture reading, and prayers, a lady with long, black hair sings passionately into a microphone, the roadside her stage, while under the surrounding fresco of the afternoon sky, her husband, the village lay pastor, strums along on his guitar, a sound as natural here as the proud crowing of a distant rooster or the rustling of long, spiny fingers of palm fronds dancing in the wind. With some final instructions on how to divide into age-groups, we begin handing out the *cajitas de regalos* (little gift boxes) to the children who have been waiting so patiently.

They must be masters at delayed gratification, I think as my emotions swell.

While dozens of youth sit on the ground in groups, opening their boxes and looking at booklets about the gospel, I step behind the fence and see a path from a small, earthen home leading down to where laundry is washed. I see a weathered and chipped flat stone, a small sliver of soap still imprinted from the grip of someone's hand, a wet and tattered garment, and a plastic tub of murky, sudsy water. A few steps below, the bathroom is a lean-to covered with pieces of canvas and a square of salvaged, corrugated steel, a common roofing material here.

One of the ladies explains to the children sitting in a cluster, "Cristo murió por nosotros. Romanos cinco ocho" (Christ died for us. Romans 5:8).

Meanwhile, the women shuffle forward in long lines to receive a plastic bag containing about five pounds of rice and five cubes of bullion. "Bendiga señora—Dios le ama" (Bless you—God loves you), the missionary lady says to each. The elderly are also given blankets. Their expressions if not their words convey their appreciation and need. With watery eyes, an elderly man says to his friend, "This is good. My family did not eat yesterday."

As shadows lengthen and the sun draws closer to the mountain peaks, the families assemble and begin their long foot journey home. Just as Mark predicted, we have no empty cardboard boxes to bring back. I watch. In arms and on heads, the tall brown boxes wobble up the road in single file, resembling marching rows of leaf-cutter ants so common here in the tropics—each soldier carrying a chunk of chiseled foliage much larger than himself back to the colony and to the waiting queen.

"These are for clothes," an elderly woman explains, happy to have one. Others look disappointed that no boxes are left, leaving me with a sorrowful pit in my stomach.

Before we leave, we assemble around the pile of rocks at the top of the hill. A mud-splattered wooden house sits nearby—dirt floor and cutout windows. Something nailed on a rafter over the doorless passage catches my attention—a small wooden cross. Hanging beside it are a couple of garments, some drying corn, and an umbrella. Several dogs sleep in the shade or roam freely in and out of the house, sniffing the ground. Through the door I see someone's simple bed—a hammock—hanging between two posts.

Bowing his head, Reverend Israel Gonzalez, forty-nine, removes his hat and begins a prayer. Israel, the leader of the area's ministerial association, is the local contact for Mark and his Honduran ministry, the Christian Community of Honduras. Others follow, touching the stones. I watch as the church's foundation is laid with prayer. An elderly campesino walks quietly out of the bushes from the steep mountainside below. Stepping into the clearing, he too bows and joins us in prayer, his straw hat and machete held reverently in his leathery hands. As we pray, I look off to the valleys and far off hills, imagining the church that will stand here one day and, like an angel's feather in a restless wind, the voices that will praise, the hands that will lift, and the music that will soar.

On our drive back up and over the ridge and down the mountain, a fine mist moves in. Someone notices that the lead truck has a flat tire. Alerted by walkie-talkie, Mark commands everyone to pull over and stop, though we're precariously close to the edge. We pile out to help, to watch, to regain equilibrium, to breathe the tropical mountain air. Calloused, experienced hands quickly replace the large tire.

Continuing on our way, we pass women and children who are still walking, even in the dark, and carrying their *regalos* and cardboard boxes. As we pass, some wave and shout, "¡Gracias!" (Thank you!) My heart aches. *Even the empty boxes are treasures,* I say to myself as we leave them behind.

Descending toward the valley town of Siguatepeque and our waiting hotel, we'll enjoy supper, a hot shower, and a good night's rest. I'm looking forward to the luxury. But I understand it better now as a Bible verse whispers in my mind. *The meek shall inherit the earth.* [Matthew 5:5]

Pondering these words in the darkness of the van, I think, *What will the night be like for them?*

"We gave out three hundred shoe boxes today," Mark says, breaking the silence, "and about one hundred fifty bags of rice. Tomorrow we go to Pimienta."

Several bony dogs roam in and out freely.

A small cross catches my attention.

The church foundation is laid with prayer.

Chapter 3

Red Light, Green Light

THIS TRIP BEGAN for me one evening during the previous October over fourteen hundred miles away. Mark Searcy, the contractor who had built both my mother's and my home in western North Carolina, had invited me to go to Honduras on a mission trip. He said I could learn more about it by attending a meeting he had organized at a steakhouse near Asheville. I knew Mark had been to Russia and numerous other countries on mission trips before, but Honduras sounded interesting, and I thought the trip might even be helpful in my quest to learn Spanish.

That pleasant autumn night, I pulled into a clean, smoothly paved parking lot filled with late-model imports, pickups, and SUVs that sparkled under the bright mercury lights. I joined the group in a private meeting room at the back. After a hefty meal—I enjoyed sirloin tips with onions and peppers, a baked potato, and frequent refills of sweet iced tea—our informal group of about twenty men and women, some of whom attended my church, watched a colorful PowerPoint presentation about how Mark and his team of volunteers were sharing the gospel in Honduras, handing out gift boxes to children and building a new medical clinic.

Along with Mark were his brother, Mike, and a business associate, Kenny Barnwell. Over the years they had made dozens of trips to Honduras. When each photograph flashed on the screen, I flipped logic into my mental boxes. It was my version of the old "red light, green light" game we used to play as children. The outcome would determine my decision to go to Honduras or stay home.

After the meeting I knew I would need more time to sort through my rationale and evaluate the pros versus the cons. Still, I saw no harm in volunteering to fill some shoe boxes. I signed up for fifty. Regardless of my decision, I could be content to merely send my boxes along with the other five thousand or so they hoped to collect from our area.

Filled with an assortment of small items and toys according to a recommended list, the boxes would be shipped ahead in a seagoing container. Of course, Mark, Mike, and Kenny hoped we would join them and help deliver the boxes in person. The opportunity sounded kind of neat. *But that's a long way to go just to hand out boxes*, I thought. On the other hand, how hard could that be? I wondered if we—OK, I—would really be needed. After all, I did have other things I could be doing, like painting my house. Retirees are busier than people think.

Not many days later, Mark and Sharon delivered a couple of cartons containing fifty, six-quart, plastic, Sterilite storage boxes with lids. Mark and Sharon are the parents of six children—make that eight if you count their two adopted daughters. A former high school standout wrestler, Mark is still as solid as the brick walls he learned to build during his high school masonry class. Mark and Sharon married soon after high school and served as missionaries in Haiti during the difficult, dangerous days of the Duvalier regimes. They later lived and served in Honduras, also.

I got right to work hunting for the various items needed for the boxes. Not being one to browse around stores, I wanted to do my task as quickly and efficiently as possible. I needed school supplies (pencils, ballpoint pens, and spiral notebooks), hygiene items (soap, toothbrushes, toothpaste, combs, brushes, hair ties, clasps, and washcloths), candy and chewing gum, and of course toys of all sorts, including dolls, Hot

Wheels, Tinker Toys, soap bubbles, Play-Doh, and whatever else could fit under the lid of a 12 x 7 x 4-inch, clear plastic box. I went to Sam's Club for the candy and to Wal-Mart, Dollar General, and the Dollar Tree for toys and the rest.

When I explained my purpose to the manager at Dollar Tree, he took me to the back storage room. With one of his workers we sorted through tall stacks of cartons and fished out many items on my list, hurriedly counting and tossing them into my cart. Almost like a scavenger hunt, we actually enjoyed finding the items and checking them off one by one. The manager even offered suggestions of his own. He was familiar with mission trips like this, he said, and offered to help again in the future.

In no time I was happily on my way. The hunt had been successful, and I was coming back with the kill. The shopping phase hadn't been as hard as I thought it would be.

Then, a couple of weeks before Christmas, my church issued an invitation for volunteers to help pack shoe boxes for the upcoming Honduras mission trip in February. Although I had already delivered my fifty to Kenny, I thought it would be interesting to see how the "experts" assemble the boxes versus the method my wife and I had devised in our kitchen. Plus, I might get to talk to some folks who were planning to go on the trip.

That afternoon I think everyone was surprised to see how many volunteers had come. There were probably two hundred or more men, women, and young people. It was almost like an old-time barn raising. Everyone pitched in and the job was lots of fun. Forming two, long, human assembly lines, one for boy-boxes and the other for girl-boxes, each volunteer picked up one or two boxes and walked past rows of tables loaded with items. Each station was labeled according to the quantity of items to include in each box, such as "two pencils" or "one bar of soap."

At various times the assembly line stopped while different items were placed on the tables, a particular age-group meeting its quota. Other volunteers scrambled to set out inventory, label boxes, and keep a running tally. One table was devoted to the tempting task of counting out varieties of candy and putting them in small, sealable plastic bags.

After a few minutes I was pulled off the assembly line and reassigned to the "shipping department," specifically the outside loading dock. My new job was to hand off cartons to Kenny and others who were stacking them tightly inside a covered trailer. They also kept a running list of cartons loaded per age-group.

I was impressed with the good planning and advance preparation for the event. Obviously, this wasn't their first "rodeo." Somewhere savvy leaders were behind this event, and they knew what they were doing. Regardless of who "they" were, it was no accident that in less than two hours several thousand boxes were assembled, labeled, packaged, sealed, and loaded into waiting trailers—thirty-six plastic containers per carton. It seemed like I was back home in no time and again feeling good about how smoothly everything had gone, how little time it had taken, and yes, the part (though small) I had played.

After seeing all those little boxes to hand out, I thought, maybe the trip organizers would need some help after all. OK, one for the "yes box," I conceded.

But then reality set in. Another meeting was scheduled after a Wednesday night church service. This time we were presented with a list of recommended immunizations and the cost of airfare, hotel stays, and meals. Kenny also suggested that we consider taking anti-malaria pills since Mark had become deathly ill with malaria after one of his visits to Honduras.

Gulp. *Uh-oh, that's definitely one for the "no box."* Score tied.

Nevertheless, I decided to go ahead and write a check for the trip down payment; I could still change my mind later. But for now I decided it was time to do some research. At home I ordered a guidebook on Honduras from Aamazon.com, and in the days following I started Googling the topic. I even carefully examined the country on Google Earth. Although I've traveled to Europe, Mexico, and the Caribbean, I had never been to Honduras. What I learned was not very encouraging. In fact, to tell the truth, it sounded a little scary.

Chapter 4

More Than You Want to Know

I T WON'T HURT my feelings if you skip this chapter, but I find this kind of stuff about a country interesting, especially if I'm planning to go there. This is information I found off the Internet mostly. Don't let it worry you too much; we have our own hazards in this country if you do the same research. When I'm in a new environment, though, I just like to learn what's out there that could hurt me. A little knowledge can come in handy, as it did on this trip.

STEVE'S SURVIVAL TIP #1: PRECAUTIONS IN HONDURAS

Diseases of Honduras[7]

- Dysentery—both bacillic and amoebic
- Yellow Fever—vaccination recommended
- Cholera—active
- Malaria—risk year-round (prevent mosquito bites)
- Hepatitis—active
- Dengue Fever—active (prevent mosquito bites)
- Cutaneous Leishmaniasis—widespread in rural areas (prevent sand fly bites)[8]

- African Trypanosomiasis—Sleeping Sickness—(prevent Tsetse fly bites)[9]
- Rabies—highest risk in all Central America
- Chagas Disease—risk especially in the south, particularly the Tegucigalpa area (an insect bite to the face while the victim sleeps).[10]
- Other diseases include brucellosis, coccidioidomycosis, histoplasmosis (outbreaks associated with guano in bat caves), leptospirosis (a rare but serious bacterium transmitted to humans from animal urine, often via contaminated water, animal, or ground contact), cutaneous myiasis (caused by larvae of the human bot fly), measles, syphilis, AIDS (high for Central America), tuberculosis, typhoid fever, strongyloidiasis, and other helminthic infections (parasitic worm), and typhus. I'll have more to say about digestive disorders of interest to travelers in another chapter.

Snakes and Reptiles of Honduras[11]

Pit Vipers:
- Fer-de-lance—accounts for more deaths than any other species of snake in Central America
- Cantil—found along swampy areas and stream banks but seldom fatal (that's encouraging)
- Hog-Nosed Viper, Jumping Viper—can strike over a distance greater than its body length (eighteen to twenty-four inches)
- Eyelash Viper or Palm Viper—lives in trees and bushes—looks as bad as it sounds—you'll recognize it when you see it
- Godman's Pit Viper—common, well-known, can be over two feet in length
- Bothrops Viper—can include several large vipers of this genus, including the Fur-de-lance

- Tropical Rattlesnake—one of the most dangerous snakes in the Americas

Added to the list of snakes are the brightly colored coral snakes (three species) with their neurotoxic venom and the boa constrictors—though nonvenomous, their size (up to eighteen feet) and strength can easily kill a human by suffocation. All total, including both pit vipers and non-pit vipers, 113 species of snakes have been identified in Honduras as of 2002.[12]

Then there are the crocodiles, both fresh and salt water kind. There may also be piranhas and the infamous candirú fish. I learned about this little menace with painful spines on the National Geographic and Animal Planet channels but it is best known to inhabit the Amazon basin. In Honduras or not, who wants to find out? I won't give the details of what they do. Suffice it to say, they follow the scent of ammonia and swim to its source—all the way.

Insects and Arthropods of Honduras[13]

Ticks, Africanized honey bees, scorpions, black widows, tarantulas, banana spiders, and human botflies, which transfer their eggs to blood-sucking insects like mosquitoes, which then get relayed to humans or other warm-blooded hosts. Once there, they take up residence under the skin. Then, of course, there are the standard bed bugs, round worms, chiggers, and itch mites.

History and Politics[14]

Next I wanted to know about the history, political stability, and safety for travelers.

It's not a surprise that Columbus named many of the places he discovered; the word *Honduras* refers to the "great depth" of the surrounding waters. He landed in Honduras on July 30, 1502, on his fourth and final voyage to the Caribbean.

Honduras eventually broke free from Spain in 1821 and for a time became part of an independent federation of Mexico. Then in 1838, after dealing for many years with the fortune-seeking Spanish, British, Dutch, and various marauding pirates along her Caribbean and Pacific coastline, the nation finally formed the independent Republic of Honduras.

Honduras's long history, however, has been bloodstained by military coups, rebellions, and dictatorships, even into modern times. Behind the scenes, foreign fruit companies wielded much control over the country's politics and economy from the late 1800s to even the 1960s. Bananas were a major export along with coffee, tobacco, lumber, shrimp, lobster, sugar, pineapples, palm oil, fruit, and minerals, including gold and zinc.

As recently as forty years ago (July 14, 1969), troops from El Salvador, the neighbor to the southwest, invaded Honduras. Sometimes called the Soccer War or *La Guerra del Fútbol,* this battle coincided with inflamed rioting surrounding the second North American qualifying round for the 1970 FIFA World Cup soccer match between Honduras and El Salvador. Not entirely about soccer, it was the culmination of increasing political tensions regarding border disputes and illegal immigration of Salvadorans into Honduras. The battle lasted only four days, thus earning another moniker, the 100-Hour War,[15] but sadly it still cost the lives of over two thousand soldiers and civilians on both sides.[16]

In the 1980s, guerilla warfare grew in the mountainous border regions of Honduras, a relatively neutral country, and became a haven for the Nicaraguan Contras. Tegucigalpa, the capital, became the hub for the Contras who were fighting in Nicaragua, their neighbor to the southeast. The provision of financial, military, and technical support through the U.S. government caused major problems for then-President Ronald Reagan and made Lieutenant Colonel Oliver North a household name with the famous Iran-Contra affair.

Elected as president of Honduras in 1990, Rafael Callejas refused to continue a treaty with the United States that allowed Honduras to be used as a military base. Eventually the Contras left the country also. Without the financial and political support of the United States, most of the country's trade shifted to countries in the European Union. In 1997 Carlos Flores Facusse became president and quickly had to cope with the catastrophic destruction of Honduras from Hurricane Mitch the next year. Mitch sat over Honduras for four days and dumped over forty inches of rain. Over eleven thousand people were killed, and as many disappeared in the torrential rains, floods, and landslides. People were literally washed down rivers and out to sea in the floods. (I remember reading about a lady who was found days later floating in the sea, miles from shore, still alive and holding onto a log.) Thousands more were left homeless and helpless. Tegucigalpa became flooded, and landslides covered entire towns. Law and order were tenuous as many, deprived of water and electricity, starved and sought shelter. The United States became the primary source of economic and logistical aid to the stricken nation, and many humanitarian and faith-based organizations came to their aid.

During my trip, the president, elected in 2006, was José Manuel Zelaya Rosales. He was to serve until 2010—or so he thought at the time. Following my trip, however, a mini-coup ousted Zelaya, who was trying to modify the constitution so he could stay in power. Zelaya went into exile rather than face the charges against him. Later, he slipped back into the country and found refuge at the Brazillian embassy in Tegucigalpa, where he is presently holed up and is trying to escape the country once again. Some demonstrations, road blocks, and labor strikes have occurred in his support, but despite the backing of the current U.S. administration, the Secretary of State, and dictators Castro and Chavez, it seems unlikely that he will return to power. Roberto Micheletti served as interim president until November 29, 2009, when Porfirio Lobo Sosa was elected president, gaining a clear majority of votes. He will serve a four-year term, succeeding Zelaya.

Natural Hazards[17]

Earthquakes are frequent but generally mild; damaging hurricanes and floods occur along the Caribbean coast.

Honduras is on the eastern side of the seismic plate called the Ring of Fire. Containing 452 volcanoes, it loops the globe from the Pacific Rim north to Alaska, then south through California, Mexico, Central America, and southern Chili. This twenty-five-thousand-mile-long fault line has been producing devastating tsunamis and numerous volcanic eruptions in the Pacific lately.[18]

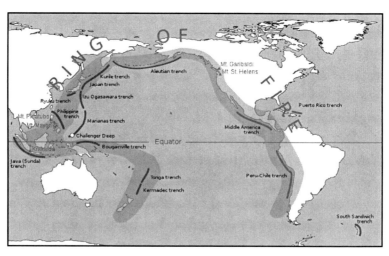

Ring of Fire

Then there's the Rain of Fish or "Lluvia de Peces" I read about. It's an annual phenomenon where (believe it or not) it literally rains—not cats and dogs—but fish. The event occurs between the months of May and July in the department or province of Yoro. Bring your own frying pan. It's not manna, so don't complain.[19]

Crime[20]

Evidently crime, gangs, and corruption—ever-present problems for Honduras—seem to be on the increase. With a population of about 7.5 million, eight to ten murders occur each day, mostly associated with the drug trade. Honduras has one of the highest murder rates in Central America. Over seven thousand were killed in 2008. According to former President Zelaya, Honduras is a transit point between Columbia and the United States for cocaine. Travelers should stay alert and stay in groups. Even as recent as October 27, 2009, interim President Micheletti's nephew, Enzo Micheletti, was found bound and shot to death execution-style not far from Tegucigalpa. Even so, according to the CDC, car crashes are the leading cause of injury to international travelers.[21]

Bonus Tip: If you are stopped for a routine traffic check or road block, show courtesy and clear respect to the uniformed officers. Do not flirt or try to get chummy with officials. In some instances, you may need to pay a fine—a *mordida* or *soborno*—a bribe on the spot. In any case, don't be flippant or disrespectful to law enforcement or the military.

Chapter 5

Final Preparations

WELL, AT LEAST I knew more about what to expect. *We have snakes and spiders, too*, I told myself as I drove to the Health Department. I was going for my chloroquine prescription as well as typhoid, flu, and "TDAP" (tetanus, diphtheria, pertussis) vaccines. Fortunately, I was up-to-date on my hepatitis A and B shots. I was to start taking chloroquine to ward off malaria, one tablet per week, two weeks before departure, and to continue four weeks more after I returned. I was given seven pills to be taken with food. Each was about the size of an M&M, though they don't taste nearly as good.

I learned from the nurse that malaria is the world's most common disease, with up to five hundred million infections per year and over one million deaths per year worldwide. (Death rates spiked significantly after the banning of DDT, affecting children the hardest.) In 2007 the Center for Disease Control reported 1,505 cases of malaria in the United States.[22] Even so, all but one victim had traveled *outside* the United States and that unfortunate individual had contracted the disease from a blood transfusion. However, we shouldn't get too confident—you may be surprised to know, we have the infamous anopheles mosquito here in the states, also. Should this small mosquito become infected with the protozoan parasite of the genus *Plasmodium*—*Plasmodium falciparum* being the most serious strain—we could experience a malaria outbreak. In fact, in 2007 North Carolina reported thirty-two cases of the disease.[23] I didn't want to be a malaria statistic in 2009.

I had a passport, so now all that was left to do was to pack for about nine days. I bought a small spray can of mosquito repellant containing DEET (N,N-Diethyl-meta-toluamide) and a couple of small bottles of hand sanitizer, adding them to my carry-on luggage—no liquids exceeding the three-ounce limit. I had a couple of old prescriptions from a trip to Mexico several years earlier, tossing in the leftovers of the tiny diphenoxylate/atropine tablets. These little babies work well for bouts of diarrhea. I checked first though, and my local pharmacist said they were still OK to use but I hoped I wouldn't need them, of course. I also asked the pharmacist to inspect an unused prescription of a general antibiotic I also had left over. She advised that in this case the pills were no longer usable and that I should discard them. I decided not to worry about getting more, hoping I wouldn't need them either. Oh yes, there's one more thing I always take on trips to Third World countries—a small, plastic bottle. It's my personal secret to survival, which I'll explain later.

The week before my departure, I went to Texas to visit my brother. While there, one of our friends, who is an officer with the sheriff's department, asked me to conduct an experiment for him while I was in Honduras. Like many Texans, Larry is an outdoor enthusiast. In addition, he seems to have an interest in survival. Well, I can't knock that—I guess we all do. But Larry likes to store military MREs and such. These small, compact, plastic packets of dehydrated "meals ready to eat" are the modern version of K rations or C rations from World War II. I didn't need them because I was packing beef jerky and peanut butter crackers. Larry didn't give me his precious MREs but a small, Swiss-made water filtration pump because he wanted to see if it worked.

"You mean you want *me* to be *your* guinea pig?" I asked.

"Yup," he said with a big smile. "I paid over two hundred dollars for it, so it oughta work. Plus, it's made in Switzerland just like my Swiss Army knife."

"Yeah, well, I've got a cuckoo clock that was made in Switzerland, too," I said. "Let me see how big it is. If there's room in my luggage, I'll think about it. But no promises."

"Aw, it ain't *that* big," he said, wiping dust off the box. "It ain't no bigger than a bom—"

"A what?"

"Nothing. I said I'm sure it works. I paid over two hundred dollars for it."

"Right, that's why you want *me* to test it out for *you*. Well, if I have a sudden urge to die from dysentery, I may give it a try." I began to wonder if we were really friends. But on the other hand, I began thinking: If there was no other way to get clean water, maybe this would

Larry's pump: "Exhibit A"

29

be a possible alternative to dying of thirst. But still, if given the choice, I would rather die from a poison dart than from diarrhea. And can you really trust the box labels these days?

"Gimme the box," I said. "If I die, let this be entered into the court record as 'Murder Weapon—Exhibit A.'"

Speaking of contingencies, I checked the Web site of the U.S. Department of State (http://www.state.gov/travel). Travel warnings for various countries are listed as well as country-specific information pertinent to travelers; all was very helpful. They recommended registering with them before going to Honduras and provided a convenient online form to do so. I typed in the length of my stay, where and with whom I would be staying, the phone numbers by which I could be reached, and my next of kin.

I photocopied my passport should mine get lost or stolen. I also recorded the addresses and phone numbers of the U.S. embassy in Tegucigalpa and the consular agency in San Pedro Sula plus all other contact information I had on our hosts, the hotel where we would stay, and my passport number. I left copies of these documents at home with my wife and gave a set to Kenny after arriving in Honduras. I also kept copies with me at all times should I ever get separated from the group. Again, I hoped this information was something no one would need, especially my next of kin.

As a trade for testing out his water filter, Larry said that if I got kidnapped, he would organize a search and rescue team and come after me. I told him to bring along Dog the Bounty Hunter and Chuck Norris. He promised he would, and to this day I believe he would have done so—not necessarily for me but mostly for his Swiss water filter.

Chapter 6

"Welcome to Honduras, Señor"

DAY 1: TO CHARLOTTE AND SAN PEDRO SULA (SATURDAY, FEBRUARY 14)

THE DAY OF departure has finally come, and I find myself at the Charlotte International Airport, joining up with Kenny Barnwell and a married couple from my church. It's before sunrise on Saturday, February 14. It's still quite dark outside.

I leave my car in a huge parking lot and take the shuttle to the terminal. I hide an extra set of keys on the outside of the vehicle—actually underneath. I also write down the lot and row

Kenny Barnwell, our good-natured guide.

numbers of my parking spot in my journal and on a small card in my wallet. Nine days later, I will be glad I took both precautions. I'll call my wife later and tell her where to find the keys and the car should, uh . . . well, you know—should something happen.

Kenny, a good-natured real estate broker, has been to Honduras more than twenty times. So many times, in fact, that he's lost count, he says. He has an endearing laugh and a heart like a golden delicious apple—the kind that grows on the gentle hillsides where we live in Henderson County not far from the western North Carolina Blue Ridge Mountains. He also works for Mark's construction company as operations manager—that is, when he's not devoting hours to World Harvest Missions and the Christian Community of Honduras, saying, "I have no title. I'm just a servant for the Lord." You would never know that years ago and at great risk Kenny smuggled thousands of Bibles into Communist China. I was also astounded to learn that, using the prevailing winds, he and his companions had sent helium-filled balloons tied with Scripture verses and tracts over the demilitarized zone into North Korea.

The four of us change planes in Atlanta and join up with more in our group as we board. Our next stop will be San Pedro Sula, the industrial capital of Honduras, located near the Caribbean coast. The trip gives me several hours to think about and absorb what I was doing and why. I notice that several others on the packed 737, wearing matching blue T-shirts and anxious smiles, seem to be on a mission trip just as we are. Our T-shirts are bright orange and are labeled on the front *CCH—Comunidad Cristiana en Honduras, Lajas, Taulabé*.[24] On the back is a Bible verse—"Les Dijo: Vayan por todo el mundo y anuncien las buenas nuevas a toda criatura. El que crea y sea bautizado sera salvado,' Marcos 16:15–16"—in small print, of course.[25]

Cool, I think, *there's my granddad's favorite verse.* The flight safety instructions are given over the intercom, first in English and then in Spanish, from a perfectly enunciated professionally recorded tape. I wonder if Jonah, a fellow reluctant missionary, was given similar instructions when he entered the belly of the whale. "Please take your seat on a rib and fasten your seatbelt. In case of nautical turbulence or stomach depressurization…"

After everyone gets settled back, small TV screens lower, and the movie begins. It's *The Family That Preys*. I choose not to watch—I have a book more cheerful and a window more inspiring. This experience needs savoring. I can watch movies at home, I decide. Still, I hope that my family is praying for me ("praying" with an *a*).

We fly over the Gulf of Mexico—it's rippled but seems motionless from this altitude, like dark blue wallpaper—then over fields of wooly white clouds and the emerald shorelines of the Yucatán Peninsula, Mexico's Cancún, Cozumel Island, and then Belize, formerly known as "British Honduras." It's beginning to sink in and I take a deep breath—I'm really on my way, but where and to what?

Reading my new guidebook on Honduras, I learn that Central America could be described as a land bridge or isthmus between North America and South America. Generally ascribed to be south of Mexico and north of Columbia, the area includes the Panama Canal—its narrowest point—where only thirty-one miles separate two oceans. This long isthmus of about twelve hundred miles resembles a tapered thread ready to snap. I hope it doesn't while I'm here.

After about three and a half hours the flight attendants hand out immigration forms for us to hurriedly decipher and complete. As the speaker boxes chime, we dutifully raise our seat backs and tray tables to their "full upright position." The jet responds with flaps lowering and landing gear locking as we approach the shoreline of Honduras.

Looking out my window, I see a muddy brown river slithering like a boa through flat green vegetation and vast coastal plantations. I remember examining this river, Río Ulúa, on Google Earth. It's emptying its belly into the crystalline Caribbean with a continuous earthy plume of suspended shock and unimaginable pollution, I suspect. We're quickly descending over curious crops and neatly planted orchards and fields on the outskirts of the city. I can only guess as we pass over—bananas, palms, pineapples, avocados, sugar cane. The verdant valley, about twenty miles from the coast, is rimmed by distant, beckoning mountains.

Pilots say, "A good landing is one you can walk away from." When the wheels touch, engine thrust reverses, and the spoilers rise, I say under my breath, "Amen." Although San Pedro Sula's "Aeropuerto Internacional Ramón Villeda Morales" is the busiest runway in Honduras, I can see that it's no JFK or Hartsfield-Jackson, despite its impressive name. A relic DC-3 sits on the tarmac, but ours is the only commercial jet taxiing to the small terminal that seems asleep in the hot midday sun. With an elevation of only ninety-one feet, the terminal was completely submerged during the flooding of Hurricane Mitch in 1998. Since then it has been renovated, and expansion is still underway.

We follow like sheep inside to the ground floor immigration line, which is long and moves like a Galapagos turtle. I learn that many of those in line—the ones with the blue T-shirts—are with a dental missions group from the States. They're rolling hard-shell medical cases stenciled with names of clinics and physicians. Others appear to be natives returning home for business or to visit relatives. I talk to a friendly Honduran who is a cook on an oil rig in the Gulf and is coming to visit his mother. About eleven on this flight are in our group from North Carolina, but we will be joined by others later as we make our way to the hotel a couple hours away.

We learn that the processing is delayed because several immigration officers have taken Valentine's Day off. At first I'm surprised, but then I try to look casual when I hear a little voice inside me whisper, *It's not just an American celebration, dummy!* (In fact, Pope Gelasius declared February 14 Saint Valentine's day way back in A.D. 498.) I hope my embarrassment will fade because it's finally my turn to get my passport stamped.

Oh boy, I think, walking up to the counter. *I can practice my Spanish now and maybe even impress the immigration lady.*

"Buenos dias" (Good day), I say in my best and most cordial Spanish, thinking, *I bet this is the way Ernest Hemingway did it.*

"Welcome to Honduras, sir," the attractive lady says in perfect English, smiling. *Stamp. Stamp.* "Next!"

"Gracias," I whimper. She could have at least said, "Señor."

Picking up our luggage, we head for the front door and the loading area outside. It's here that we're met with our first blast of humid, tropical heat. Then a swarm of cab drivers and money changers—overly anxious men with fists full of cash—descend on us, eager to swap U.S. dollars for lempiras, the official Honduran currency. Lempiras are named after the Lenca tribal warrior Lempira, who fought against the Spanish conquistadors in 1539 and was killed. The exchange rate is something like nineteen lemps—designated "Lps" on price tags—to one dollar. Chief Lempira is portrayed on the obverse of the one lempira note (worth five cents) with the Mayan ruins at Copán on the reverse. Coins come in one, two, five, ten, twenty, and fifty centavos and are hardly worth the effort—a fifty centavo piece, for example, is worth about 2.5 cents.

The one-lempira note is worth about five cents.

Our five-member team of mission leaders, including Kenny and Mark, are busy curbside, jockeying for parking places, loading luggage, sweating, providing introductions, and helping us exchange currency as others seek an oasis of shade, a premium around the terminal entrance. Our hosts and drivers for the coming week are Mark and Mike Searcy, Kenny Barnwell, Rev. Israel Gonzalez, and his son, Faríd Gonzalez. Finally loaded into the backs of the pickups, our luggage is securely tied under a curious web of rope, and everyone picks a driver, a vehicle, and a seat as engines crank. Since I know Mark best, and there seems to be plenty of available seats, I hop into the front passenger seat of his silver Nissan passenger van. I soon learn why Mark had more than one seat vacant. We'll pretty much keep this seating arrangement for our entire stay, though there will be a few memorable exceptions I'll mention later.

The seventy-eight-mile ride to Siguatepeque, the location of our hotel, is—shall we say—interesting. In places the road would serve as an excellent washboard for those who may remember them. Our overkill with the ropes in tying down the luggage is beginning to make more sense now. We swerve on the shoulders and cross the center lines. We dart around and pass other vehicles on hills and blind curves, oblivious to the heavy traffic and break-neck speed of mostly commercial vehicles and large dump trucks. Probably noticing my interest in the rear tire tread of the transfer trailer truck in front of us, Mark explains some of the discomforting "rules of the road." All the while, we new arrivals try to look like seasoned travelers and veterans of faith. I'm not so easily fooled. It's clear to me that he's trying to put us at ease.

"Here, when you make a left turn, it would be suicide to stay in the center with your turn signal on," he says. "You best pull over to the right on the shoulder and, when it's clear, go for it. Just be sure nobody's coming or passing, or you'll end up as a greasy spot on the road. Speaking of passing, blowing your horn means 'I'm coming around.' Flashing your lights means 'I'm willing to die for this.'"

36

"Welcome to Honduras, Señor"

"What does it mean when you blow *and* flash?" I ask, feeling much more relaxed already. "Like I saw you do a while ago—that is, before I closed my eyes and started praying."

"Ha! Blowing *and* flashing means 'Houston, we've got a problem,'" he says with a devilish chuckle.

I turn and look at the unsmiling faces behind me. It could be my imagination, but they no longer seem nonchalant. In fact, they look rather blanched. This might be fun, after all. I decide not to mention that I once taught driver's education, but start keeping a mental grade sheet for Mark's driving. I do, however, factor in the "when in Rome" quotient. Settling back in my seat, I tell myself, "We all have to go, sometime."

Once in Siguatepeque, our caravan pulls into a pizza restaurant. Fortunately, bathrooms are available though crowded. It has been a long drive. We're all hungry from a day of traveling, and the prospect of food, especially something familiar, is an encouragement and a spirit lifter. Perhaps in the back of my mind I thought we would be eating caterpillars and guinea pigs for lunch. Too much Travel Channel, I guess.

We're joined by a young lady, Beth Bergstrom, who will be with us the entire week, serving as our translator and one of the Bible teachers for the children. She quickly gets to work and helps us order our meal, a variety of large pizzas. Once we're seated, anxieties begin to wane. We talk, laugh, and introduce ourselves. The restaurant is bustling but delightfully air-conditioned, and the waiters stay busy bringing us refills of cold drinks. The pizza disappears quickly, too.

Back on the busy highway that seems more like a racetrack, Mark announces that in a few miles we'll be taking a detour before going to our hotel near Siguatepeque. We'll stop at the medical clinic, still under construction, where the shoe boxes, rice, and blankets that arrived ahead of us are being stored. We can always use the blankets if someone goes into road shock, I muse, but thankfully, our stomachs are full and bladders are empty—at least for now.

37

Chapter 7

All Things Are Possible

DAY 1 CONTINUED: TO SIGUATEPEQUE (SATURDAY)

FOR THE PAST several years, in addition to distributing thousands of Christmas boxes to children and conducting numerous other humanitarian projects in Honduras, Mark and his unlikely collection of part-time missionaries have been working to build a medical clinic near the small town of Las Lajas, about thirty miles north of Siguatepeque, where poor people could receive treatment. This isn't the first clinic Mark has built in Honduras; he's passionate about providing accessible health care for the Honduran people. As he drives, he tells us why.

"My wife, Sharon, was on a long bus ride one day to Siguatepeque. A little campesino lady boarded the bus on the highway at the foot of the mountains in Las Lajas. She was from a remote mountain village we'll visit this week. She was trying to get to the hospital and was carrying her sick baby cradled in her arms. Unfortunately, before the bus arrived at the hospital, the baby died. Sharon felt terrible. She believed that if a hospital or even a simple health clinic had been closer, the baby would've lived. The bus had to continue all the way to Comayagua, the end of the line, before turning around. The poor mother stayed on the bus, and with her return ticket she took the long ride back home—the dead baby still in her arms."

We're stunned to silence. "Can you believe it?" Mark says at last.

As we continue to drive, passing clusters of small homes with hanging laundry, foot trails, and rutted roads, I try to imagine the lady and her sadness. I think of her long journey home, of her lonely, several-mile walk up a steep dirt road that winds into the mountains, carrying her burden, the body of her precious baby. I picture her return into the darkness of her small, earthen home. She must have been hungry, dirty, and tired. Then I hear her screaming—long and loud—shattering the stillness of the night. I shiver as I imagine the terrifying echoes fading into the vastness of a starlit Honduran sky, a sound all too familiar in the land of the Maya—the wailing of a mother's grief.

My thoughts are interrupted when Mark pulls to the right, letting several big trucks roar past within inches, bathing us in clouds of dust and dark diesel fumes. Then he jerks left, Honduran-style, across two busy lanes toward a two-story, cinderblock building. It's set back from the highway on a slight rise, a driveway of two concrete strips leading to the entrance under an attractive masonry portico.

We park on a packed bed of sharp riprap that surrounds the striking, red-roofed building, which seems to rise out of the soft, black bottomland like a mirage. This is the hip-roofed, under-construction medical clinic I saw on the PowerPoint presentation back in North Carolina. I feel odd that I'm actually here—"Las Lajas Centro de Salud"—the Lajas Health Center, I've heard so much about.

I climb out of the van with the others. Since the team leaders are occupied, I wander about, feeling more like a spectator than a participant. But I *am* here. Touching the rough, concrete walls to assure me that this is real and not a dream, I'm reminded of my shortsighted faith and how this all came about.

Constructing the medical clinic in the remote Honduran mountains has been a slow, difficult project. As the trips to Honduras became more frequent and projects expanded, Mark and his men of action formed a nonprofit ministry, World Harvest Missions, in 1993. Later, under the local leadership of Rev. Israel Gonzalez, they established the Christian Community of Honduras. Other groups such as Indiana State University; Rivers of the World, a nonprofit Christian ministry out of Dawsonville, Georgia; plus numerous stateside churches and individuals have joined in their efforts.

Through the years mission workers have joined hands with Mark and the Honduran villagers, helping them build houses, churches, clinics, water systems, indoor cook stoves, and even bridges. None of these projects have been easy since workers have had to use mostly simple tools, little equipment, volunteer labor, and sparse financial resources. They endured frequent setbacks of hurricanes, floods, earthquakes, illnesses, and the unavailability of materials—often needing to improvise and scrounge for items considered commonplace here in the states. Military coup d'états, riots, and roadblocks—yes, even today—pose a potential and ever-present problem, especially considering Honduras's stormy past and uncertain future.

In the clinic's shade Kenny takes off his canvas hat and wipes sweat off his forehead. "Mark sent me to town one day to buy a funnel. I didn't know if I could find one or not, but the biggest problem was, I didn't know how to say *funnel* in Spanish," he says, laughing. "But I guess my sign language worked because we found one!" (It's *embudo*—I looked it up later.)

Inside I quietly walk around on the new tile in the still-empty rooms of the first floor. I remember seeing the early photographs of the site for the proposed building that night at the restaurant—a weed-surrounded, abandoned-looking concrete slab where the faithful believed a clinic would one day stand. It seemed a daunting task, or so I had thought, especially considering the location. I had envisioned a subtitle on the screen— "Mission Impossible." Well, at least it had seemed that way to me.

Then my mind recalls the more recent photographs Mark showed of workers dressed in running shoes, college T-shirts, shorts, and blonde hair falling from baseball caps as they pressed handmade cinderblocks for the walls. In the background, I saw neatly stacked piles of twelve-inch-square ceramic flooring but I didn't know then what they were. In a wide hallway that's dark, cool, and quiet, I look down at my feet. I'm now standing on them.

Thanks to volunteers and other contributors from around the States and even Canada—men, women, and young people—the dream, which Mark estimates will cost about two hundred thousand dollars,[26] is now dried-in with the second floor interior nearing completion. I look with awe at the results of years of prayers, generosity, sweat, and most likely a miracle or two along the way.

Amazed that I'm actually here, I simply stop and think. I'm standing inside an attractive, tropical-styled building nearly complete with columns, windows, floor, and roof. Someday soon it will be bustling with activity. There's no doubt now—I'm presented with clear evidence and a needed reminder that "with God all things are possible" (Matt. 19:26). Finishing my quiet walk through the building, I feel ashamed for my lack of faith and my ugly skepticism—and this is only my first day here. I can't help wondering what other lessons await me during the week ahead.

The medical clinic near Las Lajas nears completion.

Chapter 8

Suffering for Christ

DAY 2: TO BUENA VISTA (SUNDAY)

OUR FIRST MORNING in Honduras begins in a large, private dining room at the facility where we'll stay for most of the week—the Hotel Granja D'Elia. It's located on the side of a busy, dusty highway on the outskirts of Siguatepeque, a city of about seventy-five thousand. Less than one hundred miles from the coast, Siguatepeque is nestled on a mountain plateau about thirty-six hundred feet up. It has a pleasant climate, not unlike mine back home in western North Carolina. So far, no mosquitoes.

Breakfast is a large buffet, catering not only to hotel guests but also to the public. Passing through the line with my tray, I learn that *mora* is a type of blackberry or grape juice mix and that *sandía* is watermelon. When I don't know how to order something in Spanish, I simply point. The young girls behind the counter, used to such language barriers, are very cordial and happy to help me learn. They giggle when I ask if they are *señoras* or *señoritas*—that is, married or single. My vocabulary in Spanish is limited, so I go with what I can.

"Somos señoritas," they say with more giggles and shy looks.

As we finish breakfast in a dining room set aside for us, Mark starts the devotional, addressing the group seated on both sides of a long and sturdy wooden table—no doubt handmade. Most of the furniture here, especially the tables and chairs, seems to be locally made. Mark's bilingual Bible is open in front of him. Israel sits to his side, relaxed and studying our faces.

"Was Christ's suffering on the cross enough?" Mark asks the group, who sit in front of their empty breakfast plates and cups of coffee. They seem thoughtful, though perhaps in uneasy silence. "Was Christ's suffering on the cross enough?" he asks again.

Thinking that he's going to address the topic of righteousness and salvation through our own good works, I respond impulsively, "If you're talking about our salvation, yes. Christ's suffering and death on the cross was sufficient payment for all our sins. He said from the cross, 'It is finished.'" As Mark ponders my response, I'm thinking that I was too quick on the draw, or maybe this is a trick question. But I've heard a lot of sermons on the topic and couldn't resist taking the bait, if that's what it was.

Mark is on a different track, however. "Yes, that's true, but how about *our* suffering—not for salvation but *for* Christ? Did Christ's suffering end *our* suffering? Did it end our suffering for *him*? Should it?"

The group stays silent.

My mind searches for a sermon I've heard on the radio or at church on this topic, but I can't recall one. In fact, I've never even thought about Mark's question. Then he adds, "All of our lives we have been taught to avoid suffering, but the apostle Paul said in Philippians 1:29, 'For it has been granted to you on behalf of Christ not only to believe on him, but also to *suffer* [his emphasis] for him.' How much are you willing to suffer for *Jesus*?" Mark asks.

Gulp. OK, I know that Christ paid it all for our sin and thus opened the way for our salvation, but I must agree that my first impulse is to avoid pain if at all possible. Trust me, pain and suffering have never been on my shopping list. There are exceptions, I guess, as I remember the days when freezing to death on a motorcycle, sailing in storms, or getting up at the crack of dawn to go deer hunting in the cold rain was somehow fun. But I must confess that my daily prayers always include the request that God would spare me, my family, and my friends from suffering in one way or another. That's always the bottom line, it seems—at least for me. I've never prayed that God would send me a "dose of suffering." Yes, my desire has been just the opposite.

I picture an imaginary image of me pulling up to the drive-thru prayer box at "McHeaven," the most popular restaurant on—let's call it—the "Miracle Mile" in my hometown. The restaurant is famous for fast, divinely courteous service and heavenly food.

"Welcome to McHeaven. Would you like to try our special of two miracles for the price of one today?" the pleasant voice from the golden speaker box asks.

"No, ma'am. I would just like an order of Pain-Free Living, original recipe—hold the suffering—and a bag of fried Scripture references please."

"Red Letter Edition?"

"Yes, ma'am."

"Would you like to biggie-size that?"

"Sure, why not? With extra salt. You know, we're supposed to season our conversations with salt."

"Right. Anything to drink?"

"Uh, yeah. I'll take a large God's Wisdom-Lite—you know, low cal and pain free."

"Sure. Pull up to the first window, please sir. Your order is ready."

"Wow! Thanks for the fast service! You're an angel!"

"You're right, sir, I am. That's how I got this job."

Yep, I admit it. That's been my idea of prayer and the fast service I wished it would provide.

But just yesterday—by choice—I stepped out of my comfort zone and into Honduras. Did I come to suffer? Well, sure. I knew there'd be some inconveniences, but I didn't know I was signing up for Suffering 101. So far, other than the rough roads and the furious driving, the trip hasn't been all that different or uncomfortable. I definitely haven't suffered—at least, not yet. My room is clean and air-conditioned with hot water and even a TV. The buffet supper last night and the breakfast this morning were delicious; the food was plentiful and tasty, though bearing names difficult to pronounce and some items I didn't recognize. But that's hardly suffering.

Maybe Mark is preparing us for something, I think, but it's too late now for the "no box"; I'm here for eight more days . . . for better or for worse. I take a deep breath and keep listening.

Various members of our group sit motionless; others add to the discussion, including Rev. Israel Gonzalez, a large man with a commanding, sometimes-serious voice but a playful sense of humor and a ready laugh. The leader of CCH—the Christian Community in Honduras (note the logo on our T-shirts), he has helped establish some thirteen churches in Honduras. Israel will serve as our local ministerial contact and host, staying with us everywhere we go until the day we leave.

Pastor Israel agrees with Mark and speaks in halting English, sometimes unsure of the correct word. "There can be more joy when the suffering is for Christ," he says, studying us, his new disciples, for the coming week. "It makes us stronger in our faith."

Mark translates a few words for him then adds more. "Perhaps this is not a good topic for your first day in Honduras, but how much are you willing to suffer for Jesus? How much joy will you experience because of your suffering for *him*?"

"I agree," a member of our group says at last, "but it's easy to say for those who haven't suffered the loss of a loved one. It's different when it happens to you."

Most of us know what he's thinking. I was at the funeral, and the service held at my church—Mud Creek Baptist Church in Hendersonville, N.C.—was one of the saddest I have ever attended. A couple of years ago, his son, in his twenties, fresh out of college, and still single, was driving to work one icy morning and had a head-on collision with a semi. He did not live to see the completion of the house he and his dad had been building together.

Mark nods slowly and turns a few pages of his Bible. "I certainly agree. It's hard to find joy in those circumstances, but it *can* be done. And since we know suffering will come, why not then honor God in your suffering? Yes, we can let *any* suffering glorify God. Paul says in Colossians 1:24, 'Now I rejoice in what was *suffered* [his emphasis] for you, and I fill up in my flesh what is still lacking in regard to Christ's afflictions, for the sake of his body, which is the church.' You see," Mark says, his eyes begging for our understanding, "Paul is rejoicing to be able to suffer for the church—a message that's not pleasant to hear and definitely not popular with some big TV preachers and evangelists today."

Having seen my own brother and his wife and son suffer after the hit-and-run death of their four-year-old daughter about ten years ago in Texas, I have seen how God through his sovereignty can use suffering for his glory and to exact his perfect will. That's where our faith in God helps us cope and make sense out of something so painful. For Christians, this short and often-difficult life is but a prelude to an eternal life with God. God didn't intend it to be short, nor did he intend it to be painful, but that's how life changed when man, whom God gave a free will, sinned against him. We must not forget God's sovereignty. He is, after all, in control of the good, the bad, and the ugly, whether we understand it or not. If you doubt that, just look up at the stars at night. I do.

Group members then share their prayer requests and take turns praying before we assemble at the trucks. After a short break, we pull out of the hotel parking lot and head for the medical clinic, a drive of about forty-five minutes. We spend the morning dipping rice out of fifty-pound sacks, which had been purchased by the guys in town earlier, and filling hundreds of small plastic bags. We then drop in five bullion cubes before tying them off. Others load dozens of large cartons onto the trucks. These cartons had been locked in the clinic's storage room and contain the plastic gift boxes we'll give the children. Again, God gives me a dose of castor oil, at least that's how Mom got my attention when I was little. These are the same cartons I helped to pack and load back in North Carolina—yes, the very same cartons. Along with blankets and rice, we'll take them to our first destination somewhere high in the mountains towering behind us. Mark says we're going to a village called Buena Vista. Other than a "good view," I have no idea what to expect.

The biggest truck is piled high, while Geronimo, a local pastor and volunteer, and Faríd Gonzalez cover and tie down the cargo securely with rope and a well-worn, blue tarpaulin. The smaller trucks are also loaded to capacity with additional cartons, equipment, and tables.

Before heading to the mountains, we enjoy a snack lunch at a nearby Texaco station, which offers a small convenience store and a few shaded picnic tables and restrooms. Replenished, our caravan—looking somewhat like a ragtag Wild West wagon train—pulls out.

The rice and bullion cube assembly line.

Each truck is loaded.

Mark Searcy served in Haiti as a missionary when he was only in his teens; it was when Jean-Claude "Baby Doc" Duvalier was president. Mark supported himself by working for a Dutch-born agronomist and Christian philanthropist, Aart Van Wingerden, who founded Double Harvest, a ministry that provides food, education, and health care while teaching self-sufficiency through agriculture. Mark married Sharon, his sweetheart since middle school, and they returned to Haiti together. They worked long hours for little and sometimes no pay. Corrupt officials and voodoo priests threatened them. Eventually, they had to escape in the night, barely avoiding capture and certain death by the Tonton Macoutes[27] who served under the Duvalier regime.

Listening to his stories as we drive to Buena Vista, I realize Mark and Sharon definitely know about suffering for Christ. I wonder if the Lord will ever call *me* to suffer for him. Would he do so on this trip?

Chapter 9

"Because They Love Us"

DAY 3: TO PIMIENTA (MONDAY)

THOUGH I'M RETIRED, I'm still an early riser. After my first taste of famous Honduran coffee yesterday, I waste no time in trotting over to the cafeteria with my journals, Bible, and wireless laptop. I have learned to ask, "Café con leche en una taza grande, por favor" (Coffee with milk in a big cup, please). In a few days, I'll no longer need to ask. The friendly staff of señoritas seem to appreciate my efforts to speak Spanish and are eager to serve me—giggles and all.

I sit with my coffee in various places: on the outside bench in front of the restaurant, at a quiet table inside, or on the upstairs veranda, an especially good spot. In addition to a good view, the veranda provides the best computer signal. This private morning time is great for watching the city come alive and for savoring being in Honduras. I observe the highway that will one day serve as the remarkable Canal Seco (dry canal) between the Atlantic and the Pacific.

Costing four hundred seventy million dollars,[28] the plan is that ships will be able to send their containerized freight overland by truck, rather than relying solely on the Panama Canal. This innovative Central American interocean highway, officially called the "Logistic Corridor," will run north to south and join the two oceans by passing through Honduras and El Salvador. By using two deep water ports—Honduras's Puerto Cortés on the Atlantic and El Salvador's Puerto La Unión on the Pacific—ships will relay their cargo from one ocean to another quickly and efficiently, though perhaps not as cheaply.[29] Already fully funded, construction is well underway to accommodate the anticipated increase in traffic. The project includes the widening of 230 miles of highway as well as dredging, dock construction, and other preparations at both seaports.[30]

I'm fascinated by the early-morning hustle and bustle with everyone in such a hurry. I see a school bus pull over to the shoulder to load students without using a stop sign or red flashing lights. The traffic seems oblivious to the bus, the drivers unconcerned. While the traffic keeps flowing in both directions, the doors open, and a long-legged teenager hops out while the bus is still rolling. Laughing, the agile student lets others step aboard. Then, as the bus pulls out, he hops back on, grabbing the rail with one hand. The bus bullies its way back into the traffic flow and continues its hectic route and daily routine. As a former school principal, I can just imagine the horrific repercussions, not to mention the shock of parents and passing motorists, if such an incident occurred back in the States.

I see bicycles and motorcycles carrying one, two, three, even four riders as waves of container trucks and heavy equipment roar by in rapid succession. The air is filled with billows of dust and blasts of horns—in some strange way, a syncopated ballet of friendly cooperation. Amazingly, the system seems to work.

The hotel features a zoo of sorts with caged parakeets, macaws, and toucans as well as large turtles, iguanas, and even a mountain lion. The screeching and squawking of the parrots add to the early morning flavor of the tropics and my rich, creamed Honduran coffee—*café con leche*. I pretend I'm a soldier of fortune. The *African Queen* is docked nearby, circular fans with rattan blades rotate overhead, and Humphrey Bogart sits at the table beside me, saying, "Play it again, Sam."[31]

Native toucans reside at the hotel.

Maids sweep the parking lot while the air is still cool and the sun low. The airborne dust is illuminated like fog in headlights, while other maids mop the restaurant's tiled sidewalk and entrance. The "Dry Canal" is certainly living up to it's name.

As the ladies work, the newly arrived day shift guard casually walks about with a serious-looking shotgun, uniform, cowboy hat, and mustache. He carries a relic 12-gauge pump with a silver patina, the barrel's bluing long since worn off. He's friendly enough and speaks when we pass with a nod, "Buenos" (short for "Good day"). I do likewise since I like to stay on good terms with anyone holding a shotgun.

The security protocol is similar in Mexico, where armed guards are common at places of business. They seem to be plentiful here, too. In fact, I noticed an armed guard at the Texaco station where we ate lunch yesterday. He didn't wear a uniform, but he did carry a 12-gauge pump, which must be the weapon of choice. I can see the merit of carrying such a weapon, but I wonder about the guards' gun safety skills. I notice that they sometimes walk around with a finger on the trigger, or they rest the business end of the barrel on a foot. But then elsewhere in the Caribbean I have seen campesinos slice a green coconut husk in half with a machete while holding it in an open hand. What does a gringo like me know? But please, don't try any of these stunts at home.

After Mark takes us on a quick trip to a grocery store in Las Lajas, where I noticed another armed guard in the parking lot—yep, another 12-gauge pump—we again spend our morning loading rice into plastic bags while others stack boxes onto the trucks or busy themselves doing other chores.

While tying the corners of the little bags, I think about a street sign I saw earlier in town. On a side street beside the grocery store, it seemed to speak to me, and for some reason I couldn't take my eyes off it. Probably rarely noticed, it was tacked high on a building's outside wall, seemingly neglected and nearly painted over. It was a sign marking a one way street. It said, "*Una Via.*" I liked it. I even snapped a couple of pictures of it.

Alone on the sidewalk, as I stood staring at it, its message to me finally became clear. They were the words of Jesus: "I am the way, the truth, and the life: no man cometh unto the Father, but by me" (John 14:6 KJV). As I think about these words again, I compare the sign to my Savior. *I am the One Way. Yes,* I think, Jesus is *el una via.* Not *a* way but *the* one way. It was just a simple, rugged sign nailed to a wall on a narrow street; a sign often overlooked where two paths cross but so important. *Una Via.* One way. I'm glad I didn't miss it.

I smile as I think about the sign—how grateful I am for it—and keep repeating those two reassuring words to myself. *Una Via. Una Via.* Sensing a delay in the assembly line—me, I hand off another bag to be packed.

"Hey, Steve. This bag's not tied off."

"Woops. My bad. Send it back to quality control," I say with a laugh. "I'll fix it."

A one-way street sign reminds me of the words of Jesus: "I am the way . . ."

The morning passes quickly and the heat builds. We'll eat at the Texaco again today, Mark says.

We eat our customary lunch (*almuerzo*) at the Texaco's outside picnic tables. Mark serves a variety of sandwiches, chips, and fruit; and soon we're on our way to Pimienta. We have a fresh supply of shoe boxes and bags of rice, each containing the little beef bullion cubes or *cubitos de caldo de carne* which will make for some tasty rice and beans. We also have dozens of warm blankets (*cubiertas*), which we'll be handing out—it gets chilly in the higher elevations at night. Mark answers some of our questions as he drives.

"Jesus said in John 12:8, 'You will always have the poor among you,' but when you help the poor, it will have a dramatic effect on you, the giver."

Mark turns silent as we approach a roadblock with soldiers and guns, but they wave us on. In this case, I notice, they're not carrying shotguns but military M16s with clips in place, locked and loaded.

"That's just a random ID check," Mark says. Then he looks in his rearview mirror and chuckles. "Uh-oh. Looks like they nabbed Kenny. We'll just pull over and wait for him. Hopefully, it won't take long."

Mark continues talking as we wait a safe distance up the road. "Anyway, I'm sure they ask, 'Why would rich people come here from America to help us?' But we believe they'll eventually figure it out."

"Figure what out?" I ask.

"Ha!" Mark seemed to relish giving the answer. "We're hoping they realize that it must be the love of Jesus! It's all worth it if it draws them to Jesus—that's why we're doing it, you know. That's why we're here. And remember, what we do is being done with the help of Christians like you guys and Christian churches and other organizations that care." He glances over his shoulder and sees Kenny's truck approaching.

Truck loading, a daily routine.

A big, blue tarpaulin holds the boxes in.

"Tell me," he says as he hurriedly pulls back onto the road, again taking the lead, "who would you rather be—a lost rich kid in the USA or a poor one in Honduras who comes to know Jesus? What we do—the clinics, the bridges, the stoves, fumigating homes against mosquitoes and malaria, providing AIDS counseling, building churches, and yes, even giving out these little trinkets and the rice and blankets—is a method to bring Jesus to them. We'll give out probably fifty thousand dollars worth of trinkets this month, but even then for us Americans few of the donated shoe boxes were what you could call a 'two-mile sacrifice' for anyone back in the States. You know the verse—Jesus said: 'If someone forces you to go one mile, go with him two miles' [Matt. 5:41]. Guys, these people are starvin'," Mark says passionately. "If all this experience does for you is make you pray differently—then great! And even if you never come back to Honduras for another glance, I hope it will cause you to keep your gaze on Jesus."

The truth of Mark's words begins to sink in. The clinic is really a type of *caja de regalo*—a gift box—and a testimony for Jesus. What we're doing is not about the clinic, and it's not about the toys—it's about Jesus. I'm slow, but I'm getting there.

We turn off the paved road, and the van begins to bounce like a ball. The rocky road leads down an incline toward a wide, flat stream.

"We just do all we can and leave it in God's hands," Mark says. "But we sometimes get frustrated. Which village do we *not* go to? Which child *won't* get a box? Who do we help *first*? Regardless, we just pray someone will eventually come to know Jesus as their Lord and Savior."

A member of our group, a medical doctor, adds, "And the individual we give a cup of water to ministers to us just as much as we minister to him."

"Right," Mark continues. "You see, you can't do it for the kids. You can't do it for the Hondurans. It must be for and all about Jesus. If you don't to it for him, you won't follow through."

He slows the van, and we drive through the stream, but we're on a concrete slab, a bridge Mark and others helped build. He explains that it's a "high water bridge," one that lets high water pass over rather than under. Floods don't damage it.

The road then levels out, and we go through a series of large mud puddles in red clay, passing across flat sugar cane fields and pastures in the river's bottomland. Then we climb. Pimienta, an isolated village with bumpy roads, is located high up, but at the foot of yet taller mountains, lofty green mansions that form a virtual *Sound of Music* backdrop. The inhabitants are cattle people.

We turn right, off of a cobblestone path—their "Main Street"—onto a dirt trail and pull over close to a row of buried car tires marking off the village's center of activity, the soccer field. People are already waiting, and more are coming from all directions. Young village boys help carry the cartons out to the field where they are arranged by age-group and gender.

I notice that these children smile more, are more outgoing and less inhibited than the ones we saw up in Buena Vista yesterday. Their clothes seem to be newer and cleaner, too. I see more shoes. Pimienta seems to be a peaceful, happy village, and I find myself wishing I could live here, at least for a while. Maybe I could be a teacher or their school principal, I imagine in a brief reverie.

After the songs and Bible story, the boys and girls line up according to age and stand politely in front of the cartons. They are so well behaved. We rapidly hand out the little plastic boxes to the eager children, who waste no time in clustering with groups of friends to admire and compare treasures.

Members of our mission group sit with the children playing and celebrating with them, and assisting them with their new toys. Adults from the village stand on the sidelines, curiously watching and smiling.

I see an older woman standing with a younger lady, perhaps her daughter, who cradles a baby in her arms. They're watching the children. I decide to test Mark's theory. Casually walking over to them, I shift gears into Spanish.

"Buenas tardes, señoras" (Good afternoon, ladies).

"Buenas tardes," they reply, smiling hesitantly, glancing shyly.

"Excuse me, but I have a question." I feign a worried look on my face.

"¿Sí?" the older woman says slowly, studying me.

I focus on her eyes and ask bluntly, as though I were a news reporter, "Why do these *Americanos* come here and give away these gifts?"

After digesting my question, she looks out at the field full of boys and girls—the beautiful little *niños* and *niñas*. They are sitting, laughing, playing, and admiring their prizes. She gazes at the adults who are having a good time, too, teaching the little ones how to blow bubbles, and the young mothers who clutch nursing babies. A long row of men with large cowboy hats stand in the shade by the cattle fence, watching, smiling, and talking.

The young woman beside her waits in silence. The old lady's eyes fill with tears. She looks back at me and with a tender smile says, "Because . . . because they love us."

Her words hit me like a tsunami. Mark is right—they *do* see past the glitter of prizes and free food. I need no further explanation, no further proof. There's my reason, my one good reason I had searched for back in North Carolina. I nod and say, "¡Sí, es verdad!" (Yes, that's true!)

The younger lady adds, "And they have Jesus in their hearts."

"¡Sí, es verdad, también!" (Yes, that's true, also!) I say.

They've got it—and so do I.

Because they love us.

Chapter 10

A Work for God

Day 4: To Las Llanos (Tuesday)

Our hotel, clean and quiet.   Flamboyant tree in bloom.

I DON'T KNOW about the others, but I'm not suffering—at least, not yet. The section of the hotel where we're staying is a two-story unit set behind the restaurant and away from the highway noise. In front of our rooms lies a large, gravel parking lot bordered by a creek. Unfortunately, the water is a ghoulish gray, but the high banks are lined with exotic, flamboyant trees loaded with bright orange blossoms

63

and bamboo as thick as baseball bats. The rooms are comfortable but a little cramped, as most have three double beds per room. Each has a typical hotel-sized bathroom with a standard tub and shower. I had two roommates for the first two nights, but I agree to move in with a new arrival from my church, who joined us yesterday afternoon in Pimienta. This way he won't have to room alone and it gives a little more room to the other guys.

As he unpacks, I explain some of my secrets of survival in Third World countries, such as the importance of toothbrush sterilization, clean hands, and precautions of food choices in the local economy. The conversation gets me thinking about Larry's water filter, so I decide to unpack it and take the plunge.

Called a Katadyn Pocket Water Microfilter, it's shaped like a small hand pump, which of course it is. But to the airport TSA security guards, I guess it looks more like a . . . I won't say the word, so I'll just spell it: B-O-M-B. I don't know how many times I was pulled aside and had to unpack my bag, take the suspicious looking device out, and explain what it was, both in English and Spanish, not only going *to* Honduras but also returning. "Thanks a lot, Larry," I grumbled under my breath each time.

Would you believe "water pump" in Spanish is "*la bomba de agua*"? I knew this explanation would just make matters worse, especially if overheard by an enthusiastic TSA guard who didn't know much Spanish, so I used "*el filtro de agua*" (water filter) instead. Larry is a big guy and no doubt trained in self-defense, so I'll just have to think of another way to show my appreciation for the use of his *bomba de agua*.

Anyhow, back to the pump: it has a space-age ceramic filter impregnated with silver to delay the growth of bacteria. (I didn't know that either.) The pore size of the filter is 0.2 microns, which is a plus since bacteria are larger, ranging in size from 0.2 to 5 microns, and easily filtered out, including protozoans, which are 1 to 15 microns. According to the manual, this model is effective against "bacteria, protozoa, cysts [which is also good], algae, silt, fungi, and reduces viruses attached to particles greater than 0.2 microns." Unless so attached to other particles or cells, viruses are too small (0.02 to 0.2 microns) for this filter, or likely any other, to be a reliable deterrent against them.

At the bathroom sink, I filter some tap water into a large water bottle. I'm calling this "Survival Experiment #1." But just for good measure, and until I build my confidence in Larry's filter, I add one drop of chlorine bleach, shake, then drink. *Hmm. Not bad.* My roommate watches me like I just swallowed rat poison. I can just imagine what he'll tell his wife when he gets home. Nevertheless, today, tonight, or tomorrow, I'll know if the filter worked. How many friends do you have who would do this for you?

STEVE'S SURVIVAL TIP #2: TOOTHBRUSH STERILIZATION

To sterilize my toothbrush, I obtain a small quantity of bleach. Bleach is a hazardous chemical, so I like to carry just a little in a small, plastic squirt bottle—one ounce or so is plenty—and clearly label it with a permanent marker. I keep mine in my shaving kit for safety.

Even for the duration of this nine-day trip, I won't need much. (By the way, bleach is not approved for carry-on or checked luggage. I didn't know this at the time, but that's no problem because you can easily purchase bleach once you reach your destination. If you're nice to the maids, they might even share a little with you.) If you choose to brush and then wash your toothbrush in bottled water, then you can avoid this procedure, but you may not have bottled water available, or you may want to preserve what precious little water you have for drinking.

Of course, you should *never* drink tap water in these countries, but the washing of a toothbrush in unsterilized tap water is where, in my opinion, many travelers get infected with the bacteria that wreaks havoc in our delicate stateside digestive systems. With my technique, you can wash your toothbrush in tap water all you want, but when you're finished simply dip and rinse both the handle and the bristles in a glass of tap water mixed with bleach. Just a squirt will do.

Not to waste anything, you can then give your hands a final sterilizing wash with the same bleach water mixture or save it until the next time you brush. *Voilà!* Also—and this is very important—remember to keep your mouth closed while you shower. If that means no singing, then make the sacrifice. Your roommate will appreciate it, too.

Along these lines, I also suggest that you avoid eating food sold from street vendors and small mom and pop cafés or when in local homes, if possible. Ice can also be a culprit that carries worrisome bacteria to unsuspecting tourists. Drink liquids from bottled containers. Even then, I hate to tell you, there are no guarantees in the manufacturer's sanitation standards. But let's not get too paranoid—our bodies can handle a lot. Still, if possible, eat in larger, more tourist-oriented restaurants. And don't get too brave, even near the end of your stay. Remember, you may have a long flight home, so weigh the cost of "going native." However, the more you travel abroad, the more your system will accommodate and/or tolerate, as it builds up a type of digestive immunity.

By the way, I've experienced serious food poisoning (probably viral dysentery) twice during my travels, and both times it was from restaurants in the States, proven by those with me who also ate the same food.

Speaking of survival, the first of our ranks, the medical doctor, is declining to join us today, staying in his room instead. I offer a "stomach pill," diphenoxylate, to his wife, but she says no thanks. He has plenty, of course.

After our customary breakfast and devotions, we are off today for a morning of recreation. We're driving about fifty miles to a beautiful waterfall called Pulhapanzak. Water plunges one hundred forty feet over a wide, roaring cascade. At the popular park for tourists and locals alike, some in our group brave the zip line across the huge gorge. I decline, thinking how mad my wife would be at me if I died "doing a crazy stunt" like this. Plus, I wouldn't want to hear her fussing at me when she joins me in heaven. Gosh, it could go on for eternity! (Just kidding, of course.) I also decide against swimming in the river, knowing nothing about where we are or what's upstream (I'll explain why later). So I spend the time taking pictures, talking with others who also opted out (as opposed to me who chickened out), and exploring the slippery trail to the bottom of the falls, which is dangerous enough. No kidding, on the water-drenched, algae-covered wooden platform at the bottom, I could barely stand.

Mayan ruins, mounds, and artifacts discovered in this area tell of those who first visited and enjoyed the falls over one thousand years ago, yet the water never stops. It keeps flowing and flowing and flowing. Think of all that water. Awesome.

Some of us grab a quick bite from the park's small snack bar (for me a packaged candy bar and a bottled soft drink) before we pile back into our vehicles and return to Siguatepeque, talking and snapping pictures along the way. We drive by the beautiful Lake Yojoa, the largest in

Honduras and the country's greatest source of fresh water. With a surface area of some 110 square miles, it rests in a deep depression formed by volcanoes. I see vendors on the side of the highway selling tamales and fish—big ones. Mark says this used to be a popular fishing resort for wealthy Americans in days past.

We pull over at a large, clean restaurant facing the lakeside road and eat lunch. Passing through the serving line, we point to our selections since most of us don't know the names of the various dishes unless it's *carne* for meat or *arroz* for rice. But the gesturing works, and the food is good. Next door is a butterfly museum and a high tree house several of us climb as we nibble on our ice cream treats. We're beginning to relish simple luxuries we used to take for granted back home. In only four days, we're starting to miss the things we gave up to be here. It's here that I feel a little squeeze of homesickness, too. I don't know what triggered it, but maybe it's because we seem so far away or the ice cream so luxurious.

After a quick break back at the Hotel Granja d'Elia in Siguatepeque, we return to the clinic to load up for another excursion into the mountains. This afternoon we're going to Los Llanos (the plains).

Driving ever upward past washed-out ravines, Mark explains how he finally figured out how best to distribute food and other items to avoid causing a riot with people pushing and shoving. "I call it the '*boleto* method' or 'ticket method,'" he says. "I got the idea one day while reading about Jesus feeding the five thousand. Jesus directed the people to sit on the ground, *then* the disciples distributed the fish and bread to them. I first tried this method when we distributed food following Hurricane Mitch in 1998; I was worried someone on our team would literally get killed in a food riot."

Mark goes on to explain that by first giving out tickets rather than food, he avoided a mad, violent rush of pushing and shoving. Strangely, people would wait patiently in line for a ticket. Then, once they received a ticket, they would calmly go to another line to receive their allotment of food. The ticket was a psychological assurance to them that their request for food would be honored. This eliminated the panic and the "first-come, first-served" mentality. "Sometimes with large groups of children, I use the *boleto* method with them, too. It works like a charm," he says with a chuckle, keeping his eyes focused on the rough road ahead.

"Too bad we can't take it one step farther and do what Jesus did with the five loaves and two fish," I add.

"Amen," he says, laughing.

Pulling into the little village, I don't see any "plains" as the little town's name would indicate, unless it's the small and narrow soccer field below us. The name, Las Llanos, is curious to me. I'm thinking maybe they took a lesson in optimism, or perhaps it was just good marketing, from John II of Portugal in the late 1400s. He changed the name of South Africa's "Cape of Storms" to "Cape of Good Hope." Nevertheless, I see very little flat land as we pull to the edge of the road by the school.

Children are waiting. More arrive onto the field as we unload and prepare for the Bible lesson, songs, and box distribution. Every location requires a different setup, but the logistics are about the same each time—boxes clustered by age and gender, volunteers holding signs so the children know where to go, crowd control, doors locked, and nothing left unattended.

The children of Las Llanos hear the gospel.

As the children hear a gospel message from Pastor Israel and open their gifts, I wander over to the little school through a chain-link fence and take a closer look. Nestled on the side of the town's steep slope, it has two classrooms in two small buildings that face each other: one for the younger children and one for the older. The principal, a young man named Señor Wilder Smith Padilla, shows me his office, which also serves as his living quarters, next to one of the classrooms. Next to this is a small storage room with supplies and food—mostly bags of cornmeal—for emergencies, he explains.

Pastor Israel Gonzalez

Señor Padilla introduces me to Felípe, the town's deacon. The only minister is a circuit priest who comes only twice a year, mostly for baptisms and confessions, Felípe tells me. He laughs when I say, "Los Llanos must be a good village with very little sin if the priest is needed only two times a year!" I have found that good-natured humor is appreciated, though Mark says that sarcastic remarks intended to mock or deride are not used in poor cultures. *We could do without them in our culture, too*, I think.

Without my asking, Felípe says, "What you are doing is a good work—good for the children—but it's a work for God principally." Again, Mark's purpose is confirmed. God is teaching and I'm learning. I agree with Felípe and thank him.

Not long ago a young man recognized Mark and Kenny on a city street in San Pedro Sula and told them that he remembered their coming to his remote mountain village when he was just a little boy. Years later he was now able to say thank you to the missionaries in person. He told Mark and Kenny about how poor his family was and about how much the toys had meant to him and his parents. They were never able to buy such things for him. I'm seeing how this ministry is having an impact on the lives of many people—quietly, humbly, and faithfully. *Cast thy bread upon the waters* (Eccles. 11:1 KJV), I'm thinking, is so true.

I notice that many of the Las Llanos people bear interesting, even exotic, facial features and rich, tanned hues of mahogany-smooth skin. I wonder if the blood of the Maya still flows in the veins of these gentle, intelligent, and kindhearted people. Just now, I stop to listen. Pastor Israel introduces our church group from North Carolina to the villagers over a portable bullhorn that thunders across the field. He says we are from the *Iglesia "Mood" Creek en Carolina del Norte en Los Estados Unidos*. (The *u* sound of English is pronounced *oo* in Spanish.) He sees us laughing at his pronunciation. So, watching our reaction each time, he tries again and again to get it right: "Mood Creek, Mood Creek." Again, we laugh but try to help him out: "*Mud* Creek, *Mud* Creek!" we shout from the sidelines. Learning a language works both ways. It can be lots of fun but sometimes embarrassing.

Mark told us about a church service one evening where a local pastor asked a missionary lady from the States to say a few words to the congregation. She knew only a little Spanish, and it took some coaxing from the pastor before she finally and reluctantly went to the platform. Now I must explain: when learning a foreign language, some words are called "false cognates." This means they don't mean what they sound like in the other language and don't have the same etymological origin. For example, *embarazada* does *not* mean "to be embarrassed," but this lady forgot that. Standing at the microphone, she said in Spanish, "I am very pregnant, and it's all the pastor's fault!" I bet it was a long time before she overcame her red face. The proper word she should have used is *avergonzado*. Nevertheless, such embarrassment is a guaranteed way never to forget the meaning of a word. I must admit, I've made the same mistake with that and other words, but those are stories for another time.

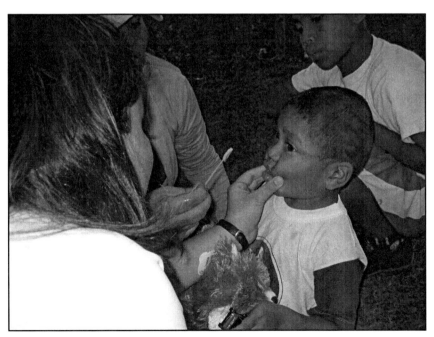

Blowing bubbles, a first-time experience for many.

Fun in any language.

Chapter 11

Living Water

DAY 5: TO TAULABÉ, EL DIVISO, AND RÍO BONITO (WEDNESDAY)

FOR ME THE van is like a classroom. I look forward to the conversations and to learning from Mark and the others. This morning we're driving to Taulabé, a small town about thirty miles away to meet Israel's wife Floripe, who is a physician and works at a clinic there. On the way, a volunteer in our group tells Mark about our encounter with an American missionary last night at a pizza restaurant. Like her, he was also a veterinarian. The man told her he was providing veterinary services for the ranchers and farmers in the surrounding villages. He explained that tending to their horses and cattle was an effective way to reach the men as he witnessed for the Lord. I see the lights going on in Mark's mind. She's getting excited too and explains how unusual it was that this was actually the second veterinarian she had met on this trip. She sat beside another such vet in the Atlanta airport, and he also shared his experiences using veterinary medicine for the Lord's work. I'm beginning to see that "gift boxes" can come in many versions.

Is it just me, or I'm the only one who thought missionaries were just preachers? I'm embarrassed to admit that my grandparents were missionaries in the Belgian Congo, Africa, for thirty-six years—my grandmother giving birth to her three children there—but up till now, I still hadn't made the connection of what they did and why they did it. My granddad preached and baptized, sure, but as an engineer from Georgia Tech, he also built schools, dams, churches, and houses. He even served as captain of the *Lapsley* for a season on the Congo River, the mission board's paddle-wheeled steamer. Hey, those were like gift boxes, too. Nowww I get it!

Mark thinks a veterinarian ministry is a great idea. "The health of a church can be measured by the ratio of men in attendance," he says. "Having a ministry that appeals to the men can enhance the growth of churches already here. We could make contact with the cattlemen's association and go from there. I'm sure we would be welcome and find lots to do."

"But isn't it weird that I've met not one but *two* veterinarians on this trip?" she says. "Is that a coincidence or what?"

"No, I believe it's a divine appointment," Mark responds. "There's providence, and there's coincidence. I believe this one's providence," he says with a grin.

"I would like to provide wheelchairs," someone else in our group adds, "like for that man we saw at the filling station the other day." I saw him, too. The poor fellow was rolling his dilapidated chair around on the rims—the rubber long since worn off. We start a collection for him then and there, passing the hat.

The conversation is interrupted when we arrive at the busy little town of Taulabé and find a spot to park near Floripe's clinic, one that was established with the help of the late Dr. Randall Williams of Hendersonville, North Carolina, and other stateside mission efforts. In fact, the building is named in his honor. It's a surprise to see his name on the clinic sign in this remote little town in Honduras, of all places. We were in Lions Club together years ago, and I was a patient of his, but back then I didn't know about his involvement in foreign missions, or maybe I just wasn't listening.

We walk up the steps through the waiting room to meet Floripe, who is finishing with a patient. A couple of women are sitting with small children and glance at us curiously as we crowd into the back room of the small building. Floripe welcomes us into her office. Setting her stethoscope on top of her desk, she smiles and warmly shakes each hand as we introduce ourselves and snap pictures. She is wearing a white lab coat, and her diplomas hang on the wall behind her. After exchanging pleasantries, we learn that she and other physicians will divide their time between this and the new clinic at Las Lajas. Their prayers are for physicians from the States, Canada, and other countries even, to come and help out from time to time. The Las Lajas clinic will focus on pre-natal, ob-gyn, pediatric, and dental services. [32] Mark adds that when completed, the clinic will include dormitory rooms and a cafeteria to accommodate the visiting physician-missionaries.

Floripe's Clínica Médica in Taulabé

Dr. Floripe Hernández, MD.

After our visit with Floripe in Taulabé, we make the short drive to Las Lajas to load boxes for this afternoon. We'll grab a quick picnic lunch at "El Restaurante Texaco" again, then hit the road for El Diviso. Mark wants to show us a few projects, like a new church they've recently built and the village's new water system.

As our caravan climbs the inevitable mountain road, children run out of their huts and yards shouting, "¡Hola! ¡Candee!" Some of the guys in the other vehicles pause briefly to hand out lollipops and bubblegum before leaving the children in our dusty wake to scurry about with bulging cheeks and smiling faces.

As we drive up to a wider and more level place in the road and stop, I see the church. Although I see no stores or stoplights, to say the least, I conclude this must be the town of El Diviso. A couple of donkeys loaded with firewood walk past, led by two small boys. Climbing out of the van, I feel like I've stepped into another century. Two more boys walk past with large bundles of firewood, except they have no donkeys—they're carrying the wood on their backs. Smaller children from the houses above scamper down the steep hillside to greet us, and they too ask for candy.

One boy, about twelve years old, is limping badly and points to his foot. He asks us to look at it. "Much pain," he says in Spanish. We perch him on the truck's lowered tailgate and call the physician to come and examine him. The boy says he dropped a big rock on his foot. The top and side of his foot are swollen and painful to the touch. The doc says that little can be done other than to keep his weight off the foot. We try to explain these instructions to the boy and administer a little TLC the best we can, followed with a dose of extra candy.

Here is a perfect example of how the new clinic in Las Lajas will help the villagers. Had it been ready, the doctor could have given the boy an X-ray followed by a proper diagnosis and treatment. I feel bad that we couldn't help him any more than we did.

Mark calls us to attention and says he wants to show us the village water system. Following him, we hike up the road passing the church and then hobble down a steep and eroded trail toward a wet ravine containing a large concrete cistern dripping with water. I begin to notice an unusual metallic sound, a rhythmic *tap-tap-tap* vibrating from the valley below. The sound is being transmitted through a steel pipe. I see that it connects to the base of the cistern. The vibrating pipe appears to follow the bed of a meandering stream, disappearing downhill through dense foliage. Mark explains that the pipe leads down to the village's "ram pump," the source of the continuous tapping sound. In the past villagers had to walk to this spring and carry their water out by hand. Costing them many hours per day, the task was a never-ending chore. The difficult task of carrying heavy containers up and down the steep, slippery mountainside was often relegated to the children. Now each house in the village has running water, even the houses high above the spring. I'm getting curious now to see how this thing works.

Mark leads us to the spring.

Continuing the tour and his explanation, Mark walks us farther downhill, roughly following the route of the two-inch steel pipe. He wants to show us where the tapping sound is coming from and how the pump works. It's a hydraulic ram pump, he says, crediting his dad for the idea. This type of pump, I've since learned, was used in ancient Egypt, China, India, Greece, and Rome. The earliest force pumps date to 300 B.C. in Greece and are among the oldest of our machines. In fact, next to electric motors, pumps of various types are the second most commonly used kind of industrial equipment today. Even Larry's water filter is a pump, for crying out loud. (I'll include this history lesson when I give him a piece of my…uh, evaluation.)

Explaining how the ram pump works is another matter, but in simple terms the water that flows freely into the pump by gravity is pressurized by using a "water hammer" effect so it can be pumped and lifted to the large concrete reservoir constructed above the village. From there the water is distributed to the village houses below with ample pressure. All this is accomplished by using some of the energy from the pump's in-coming water volume; as a result, some water is lost to gain the energy to lift it. Hope this makes sense, but that's about all I understand.

Anyhow, the pump works night and day. The only drawback I can see is the constant *tap-tap-tap* of the water hammer in the pump. There is only one house nearby, but the noise is probably a small price to pay for an unlimited supply of clean, cool running water. Remember, no electricity is used; trust me, some amazing engineering went into this system. Mark explains the physics involved and how they overcame the many obstacles in its construction. My esteem for Mark Searcy, his fellow missionaries, and the villagers who helped build this system reach new heights. His dad deserves a lot of credit, too.

While Mark is stooped inside the cinder block pump house explaining the process, I'm distracted and then touched as I watch an elderly lady do her laundry. On top of a typical and probably ancient stone table, she scrubs each garment vigorously by hand with a brush and a sliver of soap. It's definitely hard labor but a task made easier with the piped-in water. The overflow from the pump, I realize, is a blessing in more ways than one. It's a legacy of many passionate missionaries and, as the pump continually taps to the rhythm of a beating heart, it reminds me of Christ's living water.

The ram pump's water hammer.

The reservoir high above the village.

Doing laundry with clean water from the pump.

Next Mark leads us back up the trail to meet the local pastor, who will show us inside the new church. He unlocks the door and we step inside. The place is clean, quiet, and airy with open, louvered windows. The floor is made of concrete. Studs and rafters showing, the walls and ceiling are bare. I see no paneling, no stained glass, no padded pews, yet to me the place is holy in its simplicity and purpose.

The pews are two rows of simple, green-painted wooden benches. The platform chairs are plastic, and the backdrop is made of laced tablecloths with plastic flowers draped about.

Holy in its simplicity.

Electricity for the PA system.

Lights for evening services.

The mountain village of El Diviso.

When I notice two gas lanterns by the pulpit and a twelve-volt car battery hooked to the PA system with alligator clips, I remember that the village has no electricity. There are no hymnals, pew Bibles, or chandeliers. No altar or baptismal font. We take so much for granted back in the States. Back home we're so comfortable, so insulated, and oh so spoiled. To us, hardship is a rainy Sunday morning, and suffering is when the collection plate comes around. I wonder . . . if we had less, would we serve God more?

Chapter 12

"¿Mas Café o Niños?"

DAY 5 CONTINUED: TO RÍO BONITO (WEDNESDAY)

Closely resembling Pancho Villa, the author gets chummy with the guard
(not recommended). P.S. This photo almost cost me my ride to Río Bonito!

FOLLOWING OUR CUSTOMARY lunch at the Texaco station, I start cutting up with the security guard, asking about his shotgun and getting my picture taken with him—me acting macho and all, like I was General Pancho Villa, minus the sombrero and bandoliers. I don't, however, recommend doing this with uniformed officers or soldiers, especially if they're not smiling. Well, next thing I know, the caravan is pulling out and so is my seat in Mark's van. The worst part is, I'm not in it!

Oh, now I know why the guard was smiling. *Uh-oh.* Suddenly, I remember something Mark said during our trip from the airport five days earlier: "With just about every group, I have to leave somebody behind to remind them to be on time. After that they watch me. When they see me get in my truck, they come running."

Ha ha, that's funny, I thought at the time. But now I realize his words must have been a subtle warning. But were they directed to me? I just didn't think getting left behind would happen; at least not with my new "situational awareness" skills my son has tried to teach me. He's an Army officer due to return from Iraq soon. I guess I need more training but don't worry, I can take a joke. Maybe it's just my turn to be the teacher's example—well, OK, make that the class dunce. I also know Mark well enough to know that he's just messing with me, all in good fun.

A truck full of grinning guys passes by as I stand bewildered and wondering what to do. I watch the van disappear. I'm sure the security guard behind me is really laughing now ("Crazy gringos," he's thinking.) Since no one in the other vehicles is stopping to open a door or to offer me a seat, I chase after the nearest truck rolling by, a small, white pickup, and hop on. I mount that baby like Roy Rogers on Trigger, truck still moving. I wasn't born in Texas for nothing, and I'll show 'em I'm no wimp.

After my blazing gallop, I clamber and slide on top of the truck's cargo of boxes just as they're pulling onto the highway, purposefully gunning it, NASCAR-style. I'm sure the walkie-talkies are buzzing with laughter, all while Mark is getting a live streaming audio update. With my back against the cab, I get a white-knuckled grip on the railing as they fly down the highway at max acceleration, the show still not being over. With two more trucks following and drivers who can always stop to claim my flung-off body, I try to show no fear. However, as we begin to climb and bounce up the steep, unpaved mountain road, I must admit that I think my bottom is holding on, too.

We're heading to Río Bonito (pretty river). This should be good—that is, if I survive the trip.

Sitting on the back of the pickup, scrunching down on top of the boxes and holding on more than ever, I watch the trucks behind rocking and reeling, dust flying, wheels churning. We round narrow hairpins with breathless drop-offs and steep grades that strain the horsepower of the protesting diesel engines. As the altitude increases, my ears pop. Maybe for the first time I'm beginning to feel what it's like to be a *real* missionary—the kind my granddad was back in the early 1900s in central Africa. He was a big man with massive freckled hands and wire-rimmed glasses. A Teddy Roosevelt type—rough 'n' ready, brave, adventurous, courageous, daring.

Yep, I feel like we're on a safari heading into the jungle, albeit in modern-day vehicles. OK, we're not exactly hacking our way through vines and bamboo with machetes, but still it's almost like my granddad is riding with me, or perhaps he's in one of the trucks behind me, watching. And he would know why we're doing this, all right. I would tell him, "Gramps, I got it! I understand at last!" And he would be proud and calmly say with a smile, "Yes, son."

Slowing as we crest a hill, some guy hops on the back of the truck—a hitchhiker, I presume—and hope. At least he's not armed, though this does remind me of the stage-coach robbery scenes in the old cowboy movies. But he just ignores me like I'm no more than another box of cargo.

I jump into the back of a pickup.

Barely holding on (note the tip of my shoe).

I thought about my grandfather.

This was his kind of adventure—mine too!

I'm looking straight down.

I'm looking straight up.

I see six ranges of cordilleras.

The seat with the best view—mine!

Niños (children) scramble for "candee."

A "hitchhiker" jumps on . . .

94

When we roll though the twisting roads of Río Bonito and top the last hill, the hitchhiker hops off, and there before us is the largest soccer field I've seen yet and the largest crowd. The field is green and flat, the grass short, nibbled down from livestock, no doubt. A mule stands tethered in the end zone, watching us curiously. If he's the goalie, I want to be on his team.

The goalie?

The truck parks beside Mark's in a billow of dust. I slide off the boxes and climb out of the truck's bed and onto the ground—sweet terra firma. Then I test my wobbly legs. Mark gives me his famous grin and evil chuckle (or perhaps it's his evil grin and famous chuckle), but we waste no time in untying the ropes and tarps on Israel's big truck. The cover did a good job of holding the boxes in place. I notice that the box I sat on in the smaller pickup bears a perfect cast of my posterior anatomy. My treasured box now looks like a well-worn child's safety seat. Well, it may not have met OSHA's safety standards, but it worked, didn't it?

95

Beth greets the children at Río Bonito.

Just like in the other villages, the young boys of Río Bonito are eager to help. As we unload, they carry the boxes to designated spots on the field. This is not their first rodeo either, but it's been a year since the *Americanos* with *regalos* have been here, and they're glad to see us back.

After the gift stations are set up, Beth warms up the audience—over seven hundred children waiting expectantly in the bright afternoon sun. She leads them in a song as they clap the repeated rhythm. "Yo tengo un amigo que me ama, y su nombre es Jesús" (I have a friend who loves me, and his name is Jesus). The children are responsive and enthusiastic. Linda picks up the microphone and begins her presentation of the Prodigal Son. Men and women of the village stand along the sidelines, while a small group of teenagers continue their game of soccer at the end of the field near the donkey.

Team members untie the lengthy rope.

Cartons ready . . . kids ready . . . let the games begin!

We're on the top of a cordillera on a plateau. Coffee bushes grow in profusion on the steep slopes below. Behind us toward the village, the rocky, rutty trails are lined with houses, huts, and improvised animal stalls. Roosters crow, children sing, and I witness an example of prophetic fulfillment—the gospel of the kingdom being preached to the whole world. For me, Mark 16:15 has come alive—"Go ye."

". . . ¿los cerdos?" Linda asks.

"¡Nooooo!"

Linda, our Honduran Bible teacher.

Like a choir, their happy voices blend with Linda's as she teaches into the microphone held close. The shrill PA system echoes the concerto over the remote village. Tiny homes perch precariously on the ridges like coffee bushes. Smoke from kitchen fires lifts peacefully into the cloudless afternoon sky, signaling meal preparation time—probably tortillas, beans, rice, and, of course, hot coffee. From the depths of eternity, God's message of his love has arrived. It's not a coliseum or a stadium, but neither was the place where Jesus was born.

Moisés, Jose, and Atnacio—my friends.

While Linda finishes up with the children and helps them form into groups, I stroll over to a trio of campesinos with mustachioed and weathered faces. One has a tooled leather machete sheath tied to his belt. It isn't empty. All three wear cowboy hats, though each is different. The sombrero of the man with the stylish sheath is made of matching brown leather. Nice touch, but stylish or not, I'm betting his machete is sharp enough to shave with. Yeah, I know the men look a little intimidating,

We are friends, too!

but I approach anyway, though slowly. They're not smiling. OK, Next of Kin, here goes . . .

"Buenos tardes, amigos" (Good afternoon, friends), I say.

"Buenos," they reply in serious tones that remind me of the rocks we've been traveling on lately. Their eyes follow me like the caged mountain lion back at the hotel.

"¿Cómo estáis?" (How are you?)

"Bien, bien," (Good, good) they say in unison, eyes squinting from the sun.

Lightly smiling, I say in Spanish, "Here in Río Bonito, uh . . . do you grow *¿mas café...o niños?* " I ask—"more coffee . . . or children?"

Fortunately, the oldest one smiles, looks away, then says, "¡Niños!" (Children!). The others chuckle.

I'm relieved. Whew. The ice is broken. Feeling more confident now, I step deeper into the waters with more questions.

"This village is called Río Bonito, yes? But I don't see a river," I say with a gesture. "We are on a mountaintop. But where is the river?" (¿Pero, donde está el río?)

Again they laugh, and all three point to the distant valley below. All I see is green—forested mountains, more rolling hills, valleys and far-off pastures. I assume there must be a river down there somewhere.

"¡Allá!" (Way over there!) says one of the campesinos.

"Well then, is it pretty?" I ask.

Again they laugh but give a variety of responses, from "yes" to "I don't know."

I introduce myself—"Me llamo Esteban"—then ask their names. The oldest one says, "Moisés," another says, "José," and the other says, "Atnacio." I flip open my trusty notepad, then ask the spelling. They seem pleased and cooperative. Noticing my difficulty, Atnacio volunteers to write his name; the others follow suit, but I can tell that this is probably the limit of their literacy, especially for Moisés and José.

Now it's time for my test question again. "Why do the *Americanos* come to Río Bonito?"

Smiling warmly, Atnacio says without hesitation, "Por amor de niños y por amor de Dios" (For the love of children and for the love of God).

Wow. Everyone I've asked so far understands, and there I was back in North Carolina thinking the trip was all about toothpaste and Tinker Toys. "Yes, that's true," I say. Then after a bit more conversation, as we exchange analytical glances at each other, I ask, "Gentlemen, what is the greatest need here in Río Bonito?"

Frowning and slower on his response this time, Moisés says, "Money. Money to buy food." The others nod in agreement.

I'm at a loss for words. What can I say? "Yeah, me, too" as I think about the good meals we've had at the hotel or the bountiful supper of steak tips and onions I ate the night I was introduced to Honduras?

"A good work for God"

As in the other villages, the toys, blankets, and rice are a big hit. Following the event, throngs of children and their parents make their way off the field and rapidly disperse down trails and roads, carrying their boxes and cartons in arms, on shoulders, or on heads. I run ahead and squat on the edge of a narrow, hard-packed trail out of the way and for a few more precious minutes savor this experience and watch them pass. They are such beautiful and loving people. I find myself once again wishing I could join them and experience their struggling lives, if only for a day or two. *Born here, who would I be? What would my future hold?* Shadows lengthen, and the marching sounds of many feet fade unnoticed into the vast Honduran sky.

Being sure not to miss the wagon train when it pulls out this time, I run back to the van and jump into my usual seat—inside. Mark smiles. "Another convert," he says—or did I just hear him think it?

After a few minutes, somewhere along the road back down the mountain, the caravan pulls over. We stop at a little house just as the sky is getting dark. At this latitude (14° 30'north), the sun sinks quickly, or so it seems. Actually, the sun is more at a right angle to the earth here, the result being that the sky turns dark quickly with no lingering twilight of sunset. Same goes for sunrise. It's like God pulls the light switch—*blink*, it's dark or *blink,* it's light.

The threshold of the house is perched literally on the street's edge. The señora and her family are Mark's friends and are obviously expecting us—plenty of coffee is ready. She and her daughter pass out small plastic cups for each guest as we enter. The street is a steady stream of walkers returning from the not-so-close soccer field, still carrying their boxed treasures. Many smile and speak as they pass. Have you noticed? There's an absence of motor vehicle noise here in these mountain villages. The constant roar and zoom of cars and trucks is replaced by the occasional sounds of another era—walking feet, clomping hooves, or the rattle of a small wagon hauling firewood. Just now I hear leather traces slap on a passing beast of burden—all sounds that could be placed on the endangered list in my country and be virtually unrecognizable by the younger generation of today.

Inside, we fellowship, enjoy the *café auténtico* (authentic coffee), and admire their humble home. The kitchen with wood floors and walls has been built on tall supports, though it's attached to the main part of the house, which is masonry. I worry about the weight imposed by our large group. Señora has a warm fire going in what looks like a new adobe stove, the *lorena* design—from the Spanish word *lodo* (mud) and *arena* (sand)—the type most rural Hondurans still have but, as we'll learn later, is not the most efficient. She is toasting tortillas on a *plancha,* a simple flat steel plate, beside the simmering coffee pot.

We enjoy conversation and laughter, sitting in various clusters around the house or curbside, getting frequent refills of rich, black Honduran coffee—*café negro.* Soon she offers tortillas filled with meat and sauce. Though tempted, I decline. I note that my roommate is devouring one, maybe more. I understand because we're all hungry, but in my opinion he's living dangerously. Others are also going native.

A *lorena*-style stove.

The large adobe stove heats our coffee and tortillas.

Israel and Mark finally get to relax.

The group enjoys fellowship and *café negro auténtico.*

It's a long way back to our hotel in the dark. Our headlights illuminate interesting things even at this late hour: children holding children, half-naked toddlers, and others standing by the rugged, deeply trenched road, hoping for more candy or gum. Head lowered, a donkey loaded with firewood follows the craggy edge by starlight. Because nearby land is stripped of trees, firewood must be brought in from increasingly distant places or purchased from vendors.

Though dark, the night is alive.

When I slide into bed tonight, one neatly made each day with clean sheets, I'll have a lot to think about and I'll have a lot to pray about, too.

When I'm finally in bed, I'll be thinking, wondering if maybe the Hondurans name their mountain villages not according to where they are, but according to the view—what they see in the distance, like "the plains," the "pretty river," or the "good view." Is this a clue of their perspective on life? A hopeful view toward a better and brighter future?

And once in bed, I'll be praying that God will forgive me and help me better see the Buena Vista and the Rio Bonito in my own life. I'm ashamed of my short sightedness. I'm ashamed I take so much for granted. I'm ashamed at my lack of faith.

STEVE'S SURVIVAL TIP #3: HOW TO TREAT DIARRHEA

When diarrhea strikes, replacing lost fluids and electrolytes is important, especially in warm climates. Effective liquids are bullion, fruit juices, and lightly sweetened tea. Prescription and over-the-counter drugs are available that treat the symptoms. Imodium is popular, but I've never tried it. Consult a doctor if fever or bleeding occurs or if the disorder lasts several days without improving. There is more to this problem than you think, so keep reading.

Chapter 13

A Better Stove

DAY 6: TO SABANAS DE OCOTE AND THE JUSTA STOVES (THURSDAY)

AFTER BREAKFAST, WE assemble for devotions, this time on the walkway in front of our hotel rooms. Some sit on benches or on the bumpers or tailgates of our parked vehicles. Afterward, as we're loading up for our daily excursion, my roommate asks for one of my stomach pills. Others in the group are beginning to whisper about digestive problems, too. I wonder if they've made the connection of where they've been and what they ate last night. Or perhaps the problem is from contaminated toothbrushes, unclean hands, or even singing in the shower, but I doubt it. Some accept my offer of a pill but others decline, preferring to battle it *au naturel.*

To each his own, I think with a shrug, but just as well. Not all digestive problems are the same. So far, I'm good. No suffering. I fill another water bottle with more filtered water. Getting braver, I leave out the bleach this time, and the water tastes better. But should the water contain any viruses, I'm sacrificing some backup safety. In any event, I'm hoping my immune system is in good working order.

STEVE'S SURVIVAL TIP #4: *TOURISTA* AND OTHER DIGESTIVE ILLNESSES

The name above, *tourista,* is a polite Spanish term for "travelers diarrhea." The most common ailment of this gastroenteritis condition is from the bacteria *Escherichia coli* (ETEC) or E. coli, which I'm sure you've heard about. It usually occurs within the first week of travel but can strike at any time, even after someone returns home. Most cases begin abruptly and are resolved in one or two days without treatment other than to replace lost fluids and electrolytes through rehydration.

Other types of intestinal illness are more serious, such as giardiasis, which is caused by a one-celled microscopic parasite giardia found in feces of infected humans and animals.

Another concern is cryptosporidiosis, also known as "crypto." It is a parasitic disease caused by the protozoan *Cryptosoporidium*. It is spread through the fecal-oral route, often through contaminated water, and is, in fact, one of the most common waterborne diseases found worldwide. The parasite is transmitted by a hardy cyst or oocyst that once ingested exists in the small intestines, where it infects the surrounding tissue. What's interesting is the resistance of the crypto oocysts to disinfectants—even to chlorine bleach. This enables them to survive for long periods and still remain "infective" and dangerous.

The best prevention, like in most other cases, is good hygiene, sanitation, and effective hand washing. Travelers should avoid possible contact with animal feces, which could occur for example from sitting on the ground in pastures or parks or from consuming food and water with uncertain sanitation. It's never a good idea to pet stray animals in foreign countries (for many reasons), but if this occurs, thorough hand washing should follow as soon as possible.

Dysentery is a general term for a group of gastrointestinal disorders characterized by inflammation of the intestines, particularly the colon, and is one of the oldest known in this category of disease, with written descriptions dating back to the fifth century B.C. Soldiers and sailors as late as the eighteenth and nineteenth centuries were more likely to die from the "bloody flux" than from injuries received in battle. Not until 1897 was the cause of one major type of dysentery discovered, a rod-shaped bacterium or bacillus.

There are five common types of dysentery, and these are not restricted to Third World countries. In fact, outbreaks of the following types of dysentery infect millions of adults and children in the United States annually:

- Bacillary dysentery: also known as shigellosis—the species *S. dysenteriae* being the most virulent and the one most likely to cause epidemics. Two potentially fatal complications may arise outside the digestive tract: (1) bacteremia (bacteria in the bloodstream) and (2) hemolytic uremic syndrome (a type of kidney failure that has a mortality rate above 50 percent).

- Amebic dysentery: amebiasis and amebic colitis are caused by a protozoon, *Entamoeba histolytica,* and are second only to the organism that causes malaria as a protozoal cause of death. It usually enters the body during the cyst stage of its life cycle.
- Protozoan dysentery: for example, balantidiasis, giardiasis, and cryptosporidiosis are caused by a protozoan infection.
- Viral dysentery: for example, rotaviruses, caliciviruses, astroviruses, noroviruses, and adenoviruses.
- Parasitic worm dysentery: whipworm or trichuriasis, flatworm, fluke, or schistosomiasis—the second-most widespread tropical disease after malaria.

Note: Check the Center for Disease Control (http://www.cdc.gov) for more information, including the symptoms of each of these diseases.

Today Mark wants to take us to the village of Sabanas de Ocote to show us the new energy-efficient stoves he and others have helped build and install in many homes.

Although still high in elevation, Sabanas is located in a valley and is relatively flat—a pleasant change. We're at least able to "circle the wagons" in a vacant lot, presumably the de facto soccer field. Upon our arrival, as if by magic, bubblegum, balloons, and lollipops appear in the mouths of the children. I never exactly see where they come from. Someone in our group, of course, is the secret candy distributor. I'm guessing it's Mike Searcy, since good-humored ways, I've noticed, seem to run in the family. Mike is a quiet boulder of a man, and I perceive him to be a cornerstone of support to Mark's ministry. Israel teasingly calls him "Mario" after the *Super Mario* Nintendo games. Using my own intuition, I conclude that this moniker is presumably based on several factors. First is his resemblance to the cartoon character of the same name; he also says "yahoo" frequently and loves to wear bib overalls, as does the cartoon character. Might I add a fourth reason? He's lots of fun. His real-life twin could be the late wrestler Captain Lou Albano, also known as Super Mario. In fact, Lou Albano has actually been attributed as the inspiration for the Nintendo character, but Mike is the real deal. Believe me. Hollywood agents, take note.

Mike "Mario" Searcy without his customary overalls.

Accompanied by the kind homeowner, who has been splitting long slivers of firewood in the front yard, we walk around the house to inspect their stove. It's in back, attached to the house in a covered outside kitchen of sorts. It's smaller than the *lorena* stove we saw at the señora's house last night. Called the Justa stove, its design represents the efforts of many people and scientists over the years who were challenged to develop a stove that would do the following: (1) burn less fuel and thereby reduce deforestation; (2) emit less-harmful gasses and smoke into the kitchens and homes; (3) heat and cook more efficiently; (4) reduce home fires, burns, and scald injuries; (5) be inexpensive and easy to build; and (6) use materials readily available in Honduras.

Developing this stove was no simple task since electricity and liquid or gas fuels were not in the equation. Israel Gonzalez, Mark Searcy, and other volunteers assisted the researchers in the pre- and post-scientific studies, the design specifications, the construction, and the eventual distribution and installation of many of these Justa stoves—in this and other villages in Honduras.

THE HONDURAS STOVE PROJECT [33]

In February 2007 the Indiana University School of Medicine and their departments of Family Medicine and Public Health launched a wood stove research project. Originally called the "Lorena Stove Project" the title was modified to "The Honduran Stove Project" because of a shift in the model stove's design. Research began in the rural village of Sabanas near Taulabé and was divided into three phases (1. Pre-stove development, 2. Stove construction, and 3. Post-stove evaluation), extending over an eighteen-month period. The purpose was to establish an accurate baseline of scientific data on respiratory health, harmful gases (such as deadly carbon monoxide), suspended particles, and pollutants as well as to study the construction of a prototype stove. The entire village participated in the study, some 163 people and about thirty-five homes.

The World Health Organization states that more than half of the world's population depends on the burning of biomass to meet their basic energy needs of cooking and heating. Over 80 percent in Latin America use wood for cooking fuel—90 percent in rural areas and 50 percent in urban areas. One hundred percent of the homes in Sabanas used wood-burning stoves and still do.

Research shows that indoor air pollution resulting from burning biomass (wood, dung, and agricultural residue) and coal kills more people worldwide than malaria. The main health concerns are from the frequency of asthma, emphysema, obstructive pulmonary disease, and other problems that result from smoke from the various cook stoves common in Honduras and other Third World countries. Scientists say that cooking with solid fuels on open fires or traditional stoves creates smoke that is similar in composition to tobacco smoke but actually more harmful. According to Dr. William A. Pryor, with the University of California, tobacco smoke causes damage in the body for approximately thirty seconds after it's inhaled, whereas wood smoke continues to be chemically active, causing damage to cells in the body for up to twenty minutes. That's damage lasting forty times longer.

Scientific and medical studies conducted in the country of Honduras report that acute respiratory infections are one of the leading causes of death in children under five.

Initially, the project focused on the *lorena* adobe stove—from the Spanish words *lodo* for mud and *arena* for sand. The *lorena* stove is a simple design with an enclosed burn chamber and a chimney to carry smoke out of the house. Designed by Aprovecho Research Center in Oregon, the stove was first introduced in Guatemala in the 1970s; however, it proved not to be as efficient as many hoped. Plus the chimney required frequent maintenance.

The *plancha* (griddle) stove, introduced in the 1990s, has a built-in metal top griddle and an enclosed, cinder-block body for the fire. All cooking is done on top of the *plancha*. These stoves proved to be more efficient and more effective in venting smoke out of homes.

The next evolution in stoves came with the Justa stove, named in honor of Doña Justa Nuñez of Suyapa, Honduras, who helped in its original testing. This brick-built design incorporates the "rocket" elbow for efficient combustion. Heat transfers well, and the stove has a chimney for smoke evacuation. Invented by Dr. Larry Winiarski, designer of the similar "rocket stove" and technical director of Aprovecho, the rocket elbow is easy and inexpensive to build. It has a hollow, L-shaped shaft made of ceramic or clay for the combustion chamber. The device sits in a metal or brick container, and the space around it is filled with lightweight, fireproof insulation. Through a hole at the bottom of the stove, long slivers of wood are poked into the fire and fed as the wood burns, directing the heat to the *plancha* above, not to the sides of the stove body as occurs in the *lorena* stove.

The Justa stove.

The study found that compared to the "control home" with the traditional stove arrangement versus the Justa stove, carbon monoxide in the home with the Justa stove went down from 26.5 ppm (parts per million) to only 0.5 ppm, a dramatic decrease of this deadly gas by a remarkable 2,563.6 percent. Suspended air pollutants were also greatly reduced, thus improving the health of the residents. Reports of asthma and other breathing problems have dramatically declined. The Justa stove cost the researchers about $150 in materials, including glass, concrete, and welding; although Mark has been able to build the stoves for around $115 to $118 per stove. Other stove designs can be made more cheaply, of course, though they are likely to be less efficient, less safe, and not as functional, at least not in Honduras.

Mark explains *la Justa estufa ecological*—the Justa energy-efficient stove.

After our tour, we walk around the village, look at stoves in other homes, and visit with some of the villagers. Others in our group engage the kids in a game of soccer. I'm surrounded by a cluster of girls, who for some reason want to demonstrate to me their bubblegum-blowing prowess. But soon I hear Mark, Kenny, and Mike cranking their engines. I hate to leave, but Mark says lunch is waiting for us at the Texaco, and it's too far to walk. He's arranged for us to have *tamales auténtico*—this should be interesting.

The bubble-blowing contest begins. Ready, set—"¡Vuele el globo!" . . .

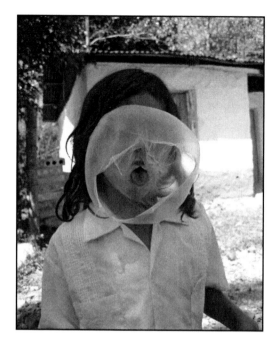

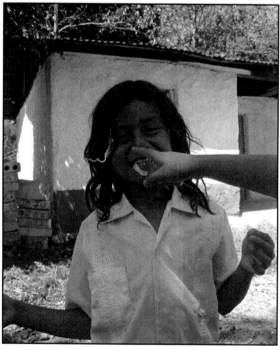

. . . and ends with a bang!

Somehow Mark is always supplied with plenty of picnic supplies for our lunches—bread, beverages, luncheon meat, and all the fixin's—and he's always gracious in serving us, even today with a tray full of rolled up banana leaves. Sorry, but I'm not crazy about tamales or their looks; they remind me of some of my Boy Scout recipes. I think those concoctions promoted in the *Boy Scout Handbook* were designed to make us young scouts appreciate Mom's cooking when we got back home. This will have the same effect, I'm sure. But I grab a tamale just to prove I'm no wimp and can go native when I want to. However, *no me gusta mucho.* I just hope whoever prepared the food remembered to wash the banana leaves. Remind me—I want to see if we're missing any off the trees back at the hotel.

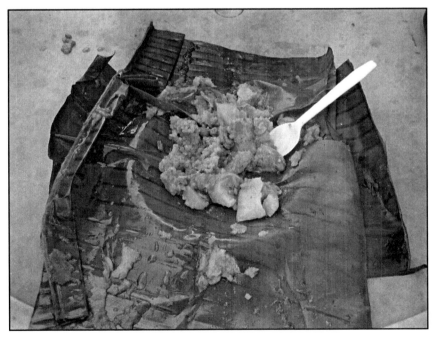

Tamales auténtico.

By the way, not far from the Texaco where we're eating is a little pink and white wood-framed building called Middle Cross Baptist Church. It has a story.

Our "*Restaurante de Texaco.*"

Several years ago, Linda, our Honduran Bible teacher, and her husband, "Ángel," (pronounced "Áhng-hel" in Spanish), were regularly hosting worship services with a small group of people, a fledgling church, in their home. They had no other place to meet.

The group had a pastor but now they wanted to build a place to worship, a regular church building. They began to pray that God direct them. Eventually, several members felt the Lord was guiding them to the vacant lot next door. How convenient! However, it was owned by a wealthy businessman not known for his faith, friendliness, or generosity, and it didn't have a for sale sign posted. After more prayer and discussion, the congregation voted to dispatch emissaries to see if the land could be purchased.

They selected the pastor and Ángel to go. They were to ask the businessman if he would consider selling the land so a church could be built. The two men were understandably nervous when they entered his office, especially Ángel, a small-framed man and a recent believer

122

in Christ. True to his reputation, the businessman was not friendly to them; in fact, he was rather hostile. The owner let them know in no uncertain terms that the land "was not for sale—no way—and not at any price."

Dejected, they returned to report back to the congregation. Perhaps the Lord's leading had been misunderstood. Or—perhaps it hadn't, someone suggested. So they continued to pray day after day, week after week. Finally, after receiving no other direction from the Lord, the congregation asked the pastor and Ángel to go back and ask again. It's here I would have said, "Lord, send someone else to do it—send Aaron!" Or maybe I would have done like Jonah, and take a quick Mediterranean cruise. But fortunately, the pastor and Ángel didn't say or do that, they went as directed.

Coming into his office the second time, the businessman still seemed angry when he saw them. Again they asked about the land. Again the businessman replied in a gruff tone; only this time there was even more conviction and urgency but with a twist: "I told you once before, the land is *not* for sale, not at any price—but…I have decided—for a church—you can have it. I *have* to give it to you—I *have* to—at no charge! Now come, show me how much land you need…."

Maybe someday we'll learn more about the businessman's change of heart, but Christians recognize the hands of the heart surgeon, don't we?

Today, the attractive little church with a brown roof sits on a rise, facing the busy highway and is the site of regular services. "Build it and they will come" may be true, but with God I see once again that all things are possible. Moses and Aaron learned that, too—and certainly so did Jonah.

A church now sits on land that was "not for sale."

With God all things are possible.

Chapter 14

A Sweet Offering to the Lord

Day 6 Continued: To El Palmichal O La Fátima
(Thursday)

STOMACHS FULL, FOR those who could still eat, we hurriedly load more boxes at the clinic and head out on yet another excursion. This afternoon we're heading to a village called El Palmichal O La Fátima. It's on the same rough road that goes to Río Bonito, the town I remember only too well due to my rough ride in the back of the pickup. My research later leads me to guess that the tiny village is named after Portugal's Our Lady of Fátima, the Virgin Mary. Again we climb the mountainous trail, but at least I'm riding inside this time and have more than a pasteboard box for a seat.

We bounce and sway from the familiar bumps and hairpin curves, attracting the attention of ever-present children who stand near their huts

Going native takes its toll.

as we pass. Our caravan soon pulls through an opening in a chain-link fence surrounding a school. We park on a grassy field out of the way, but already people of all ages fill the area in anticipation of our arrival.

A Sweet Offering to the Lord

The school consists of two separate, single-story buildings with a covered walkway and a small storage shed in between. The lower building seems to be a vacant cafeteria, and the other contains two classrooms.

The afternoon is planned to go as usual, but today Pastor Israel is playing the creation story on CD. Perhaps wanting to summon the villagers like a church bell, Israel has the volume set at maximum level, it seems. The announcer's deep voice, a Spanish basso profundo, is melodious, rhythmic, and quite dramatic, capturing the attention of many. How could it not? I get the gist of the story—the Devil tempting Eve with *la fruita* from the Tree of Knowledge of Good and Evil. The story, a bit scary-sounding in places, reverberates across the field, against the school's walls, and echoes down the hard-packed street.

Many stand under the shade of a large mango tree with its long, deep-green leaves or under the school's awning, while children play with colorful balloons in the sun. People keep coming. They come walking down the steep mountain road, babies in arms and by the hand. Others trudge up from the villages below. Faces are wet with sweat and flushed from the equatorial heat. Lofty mountains cloaked in lush shades of avocado provide the walls for this open-air church. The ceiling is merely the vaulting blue sky, but it is unmatched by Michelangelo's fresco in the Sistine Chapel. I imagine that it was a day just like this when Jesus spoke on the Mount of Olives. Yes, I think, *God is watching—and listening.*

This will be our last presentation before returning to the States on Sunday, and I try to absorb all that's going on around me. I notice the school principal keeping a wary eye on his motorcycle parked between the two buildings. Occasionally he shoos children away from climbing on it, while he helps with crowd control and Mark's *boleto* distribution. He tells me he lives in the city of Siguatepeque and rides his motorcycle to work each day. Students attend from 8:00 A.M. to 1:00 P.M., and no lunch is served. The bathrooms are the outdoor privy type located behind and between the buildings. Two of them. I dare not look.

I help the principal stretch a long extension cord for the PA system needed for Beth's Bible lesson, while others are setting up some tables

129

Children enjoy their *cajitas de regalos*
(little gift boxes) at La Fátima.

for supplies and equipment. The nearest outlet is in a classroom on a far wall, but the yellow cord is a little too short to reach through the door. Fortunately, I see a torn place in the window screen—actually behind a heavy chain-link wire. We use this convenient vandal's entry point to pass the wire. The route gives us just the extra length we need. He's pleased with this arrangement since the classroom door can now be kept locked. I know how principals think. Seeing the bundle of keys hanging from his belt triggers memories of my former career. Regardless of the country or language, school leaders have a lot in common and they have my full respect.

The children are occupied while the women form a long line with their *boletos* to receive their rice, bullion cubes, and a Christian tract. Older women and a few men receive blankets as well and seem very appreciative. An occasional balloon pops, but there are more for the asking—"¿Un globo?" Many open *paraguas* (parasols) against the sun. The afternoon seems unusually warm, and shade is at a premium

131

Inside a classroom at El Palmichal.

here in El Palmichal O La Fátima—a big name for such a small village. But soon the evening shadows appear, and the kids have their boxes opened, Tootsie Pops in their mouths and smiles on their sweaty little faces. Their parents are delighted, too. In every village, there is no doubt that parents love their children despite their poverty; these parents keep their children close. I recall Mark's question—"Who

would you rather be?" I think of some cases back home where children aren't so lucky or so rich.

Again my mind sails off on another fantasy. This time I dream that it is *my* town being visited by missionaries—Honduran missionaries. They come from Buena Vista, Pimienta, Las Llanos, El Diviso, Río Bonito, Sabanas, and La Fátima. We flock to our county's Jackson Park to receive gifts they have for us—not plastic shoe boxes full of Wal-Mart trinkets but boxes full of love. Eagerly removing the lids, we find Husband and Wife Happiness, Family Unity, Appreciation, Respect, Harmony, Humility, Innocence, Self-sacrifice, and most of all, Faith— faith in an

Opening their *cajitas de regalos* (little gift boxes).

Tres caballeros—three gentlemen.

ever-present and living God. If only it were that easy. Yes, we could learn a lot from the Honduran people, but sadly, it's only a dream. But I still wish they could come and bring *their* treasures, their *regalos* to us.

Oh well, it's time for us to load up and leave. It's been a long, hot, and dusty afternoon.

After we load the tables and sound equipment into the backs of the pickups, someone suggests we take a group photo before we pull out. We hurriedly assemble down the dirt street and stand in front of someone's house. Inside the door, children I recognize are playing with their new toys and still sucking on their lollipops. Using the house as a backdrop, a passerby volunteers to take our picture with our various digital cameras. All the while the women of the house pose and smile through the open window—a nice centerpiece for our photos. After leaving, again we see our plastic Sterilite boxes, dozens of them, happily bouncing their way down the village highways and byways, each little box a message that someone cares and that they are loved.

Señoritas bonitas—pretty ladies

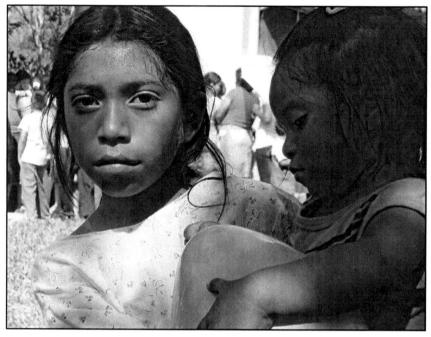

Does the Mayan blood still flow?

Beth teaches a Bible lesson at La Fátima.

"We gave out 206 shoeboxes today," Kenny says, "a total of 1,544 boxes for the week. Not bad." The boxes came a long way to get here, but no price could equal their value. For many, the little box and the simple message of God's love will never be forgotten.

As we bump and jiggle back down the narrow mountain road, Mark radios for all vehicles to pull over. Ahead I see a small church under construction. For the next few minutes, leaving our trucks blocking the road, we visit with the men who are laying block and mixing cement. A pickup with two campesinos pulls up behind. They are loaded with large, white bags of coffee beans. The driver instinctively turns off his motor and waits patiently, assuring us there's *"no problemo."*

Assembling at the construction site, Pastor Israel leads all of us in prayer, some touching the walls as he prays. The school principal arrives on his motorcycle, his briefcase tied to the back, the engine puttering loudly. He can't pass either. Wearing a full-protective helmet, he also waits for us to finish praying, though not as patiently as the coffee growers: he keeps his motor running and helmet on. After the prayer, I head back to the van but stop to speak to him and admire his motorcycle—a trail bike perfect for these roads. Soon he's able to gingerly weave around our vehicles, apparently eager to get to the highway below and continue on his way home.

Mark tells us that depending on where they live, local campesinos often refer to themselves as either "mountain people" or "highway people." For the last several days, we have made many friends with the "mountain people." I like them and will miss them. I'm a "mountain person," too, I decide, as I think about my Blue Ridge Mountains back home. Right now, those hills seem to be in another world and a thousand years away.

We're all hot, grimy, hungry, and thirsty. And most of us, I'm guessing, need to use the restroom, but the day isn't over by a long shot.

After unloading our equipment back at the clinic's storage room, we take a short ride just up the highway to the home of Ángel and Linda, our Honduran Bible teacher, and their family. Mark's friends, they have offered to serve supper to our large group. At this point, however, everyone is more interested in *el baño* . . . uh, to wash our hands.

Supper is local cuisine of barbecue chicken, tamales, rice, and potato salad. It is served behind Ángel's shop under a roof. Ángel is a sign painter and calligrapher. He also makes metal license tags for those who have lost the official Honduran tag. These are counterfeit, to be sure, but legal since the government has no procedure to replace lost or stolen tags. In fact, Mark says the police refer their ticketed "clients" to him. I figure since his name is Ángel, he can't be too bad. In fact, he's a friendly, tender-hearted, and generous person with a great smile. By the way, the little pink and white church built on the land that was not for sale is right next door. It must make him feel good every time he

Ángel's sign-painting business

looks at it and worships inside. Humm…maybe he is an "angel" after all. Do you think? Still, interesting name considering the mission they were on. You nev-verr know…

After a wonderful meal, fellowship, and the kind use of their facilities—a small but clean room with an outside entrance attached to the sign shop—we pile back into the vehicles and head off to another village, even at this late hour. I'm slowly beginning to realize this mission trip is nothing like the school principals' conventions I used to attend—fancy restaurants, banquets, entertainment, coffee breaks, comfortable chairs, early dismissals. But then I compare the results—the seeds, the fruit, the harvest.

Mark says we're now going to a church service in Ocoman. That's appropriate because it's now "O-dark-thirty," and I mean dark. I'm just glad he knows the way.

The road is the worst yet and would make a great proving ground for Goodyear or Firestone. The rocks poke up like stalagmites. I remember times when, sailing to islands in the Caribbean, I had gone ashore barefooted, forgetting my sandals, and had to painfully walk on this type of volcanic, razor-topped rock. Real killers. The trucks bounce with bone-snapping, vertebrae-compressing, whiplash-inducing jerks. I'm thinking that a storm at sea would be better. Mark just laughs and keeps on talking, telling stories, and quoting Scripture, even above the clatter of our squeaking truck and rattling teeth.

Finally arriving, we park alongside the road near the church and slither out of the van and into the pitch black night. Mark whips out his flashlight faster than Wyatt Earp. I'm trying to put my ribs back in place and start hoping this will be a healing service. Well, it is, of course, but of the spiritual kind. That works for me.

The church is lighted by electricity, and the service is already underway, a nicely dressed lady singing a solo into a handheld microphone. She's probably the pastor's wife, I conclude. Traditionally in this church at least, men sit on one side and women on the other, but they welcome us and pretend not to notice our seating arrangement and other differences. We try to join and blend in as best we can, our singing accompanied by a guitar, drums, raised voices, and lifted hands. It's a simple but pure worship to the Lord from his most precious. An eerie gust of wind blows through the louvered windows, and like ocean waves, ruffles the long thin strips of plastic fringe draped across the ceiling.

As a hefty crowd of children pile onto their designated wooden benches at the rear corners of the room, the air fills with smells of burning pine from the village cookstoves and, I must share with you, of little bottoms that have never felt the clean, white softness of real toilet paper. Still, it's a sweet offering to the Lord from those who will one day inherit the earth.

The pastor preaches a sentence or two at a time, and Beth expertly translates, not missing a beat. There's much, much more I could say, but tomorrow we leave them behind. We'll spend the night at Copán near the ruins of another civilization, of another people, and of another time. But for now I hear the Honduran calling—that's what I call my morning cup of coffee. He's beckoning from our hotel even now. OK, you may remember him as "Juan Valdez."

Even though I yearn for sleep, I decide to shower tonight rather than in the morning. It's been a long, hot, tiring, and dusty day; and it feels good to be clean again. I'll sleep peacefully—my last night in the Hotel Granja d'Elia—a long way from home, but in many ways, much closer to God.

Chapter 15

Road to Copán

DAY 7: IN THE VAN (FRIDAY)

IT'S NOT 6:00 A.M. yet. I'm on the upstairs veranda with a large cup of coffee and my computer on battery power. I'm packed and ready to go. I awoke at 5:30, ready to take another shower, but guess what? No water! Good thing I bathed last night. With no tap water, in this case I used bottled water provided by the hotel to brush my teeth but made sure I saved some for the trip ahead.

Soon, we'll be heading north toward the border of Guatemala and to Copán, where the Maya once lived.

At the risk of sounding melodramatic or giving you the wrong impression, I will share a ghost-like dream that came to me last night or perhaps early this morning before I woke. I wanted to tell my roommate but I was too embarrassed.

In my dream I was in one of the villages—I don't know which—and a little girl came up to me, put her arms around me tightly, and kissed me on the check. It was . . . well, it was a deep, long, almost passionate kiss. But that's all it was—just a kiss. I woke with a strange feeling and was somewhat shaken and puzzled. The experience had seemed so real, her love so genuine, her kiss so sweet. Did God send this gift to me?

Was her kiss a thank you in the form of a dream? I'll keep this memory to myself, and I'll never forget that kiss. I still wonder though—who was that little girl in my dreams?

STEVE'S SURVIVAL TIP #5: EMERGENCY FOOD AND WATER STASH

I've found that it's always good to have a bit of food—peanut butter crackers and beef jerky work well for me—and a bottled drink with you at all times. Have these items with you in your airplane carry-on luggage, too. You never know when you may be stuck on the tarmac for hours with nothing to eat or drink. It's also possible you could be confined somewhere other than in an airplane or perhaps even lost with no restaurants or grocery stores nearby. You can't call "911" in Third World countries nor will you find a McDonald's on every corner. So, remember the old Boy Scout motto: "Be prepared."

Also keep your toothbrush with you. In desperation I once brushed my teeth under a bridge in Cuernavaca, Mexico, and used the toothbrush later to comb my hair in a restaurant bathroom, believe it or not. Hey, don't panic! I sterilized it later. Remember, the point is to survive—be innovative, flexible, and alert. Being suave or even modest may have to take a backseat sometimes, depending on your will to survive. Oh, and always carry a small flashlight with you and, if you have room, a little bottle of hand sanitizer.

With our bags loaded, keys turned in, and tips left for the maids, we again assemble in front of our rooms on the ground level. The dad from my church who lost his son presents the devotions, his wife sitting at his side. This is their second trip to Honduras since the tragedy.

He begins by reading Psalm 30:11–12: "You turned my wailing into dancing; you removed my sackcloth and clothed me with joy, that my heart may sing to you and not be silent. O Lord my God, I will give you thanks forever."

"When I got the call that morning [about his son's death]," he said, "there were moans and groans that were unfamiliar to me. But over the years those moans became more familiar—sort of like friends. I felt like I was wearing sackcloth, but gradually the Lord removed it. We thought we were close to the Lord . . . but not like now. We sang and danced . . . but not like now. Now God has completely clothed us with joy. Don't be silent about the joy you have seen through suffering: show it, teach it, live it—that joy." Those in our group listen somberly with downcast eyes, though few, I suspect, can really relate to what he's talking about. I can't.

He refers us to the Scriptures once more, reading from 1 Peter 1:6–7. "'In this you greatly rejoice, though now for a little while you may have had to suffer grief in all kinds of trials. These have come so that your faith . . . may be proved genuine.' My friends, should we welcome tragedy in our lives so our faith will be proved genuine?" he asks. "I can't do that. But it does come. God allows it so we can advance the gospel and bring glory to him. Paul said to the Philippians in chapter one that what had happened to him served to advance the gospel and make the Savior clear. He was in chains for Christ, Paul said. And like Paul, because of *my* suffering—*my* chains—I encourage you, too, to proclaim the Word of God more courageously and fearlessly."

Then his wife adds, "Psalm 31:9 has been a support to me many times on hard days: 'Be merciful to me, O Lord, for I am in distress.' But when it came to grieving," she says, "I would often pray to God, 'Not today, Lord, *please*.'"

"Yes," her husband says softly. "I often pray, too, 'Heal the wound but leave the scar, Lord.' I encourage each of you to use your suffering to bring glory to God." He clears his throat and continues. "Don't let it go to waste but make up your mind now that if and when tragedy comes,

143

you will be like Abraham—his mind was made up ahead of time—that you will run *to* God, not away. Curl up in his arms and hang on. He loves you deeply. Then you'll be able to be like King David and say, 'I love you, God. I will rejoice forever in you and sing and dance the rest of my life.'"

Pastor Israel says, "Amen." Then he adds a few closing comments in Spanish as several wipe tears. He pauses for Beth to translate.

"The apostle Paul had an unknown problem that he asked the Lord to take away. 'My grace is sufficient for you' [2 Cor. 12:9], God said. You see, we try various things when tragedy comes, but remember my friends—God's grace is sufficient. It is even bigger." Beth's eyes also fill with tears, her voice breaking as she struggles to finish. Through blinking eyes, our glances shift from the sharp stones at our feet to Israel, to Beth, to the boy's parents, and then to Mark, who steps up.

He closes with prayer. "Lord, when we encounter tragedies, difficulties, and hardships, help us to see *you* in it. Amen."

With these somber thoughts, our group breaks up. We sense another transition in our lives. I can see it on our faces, in our eyes—a reluctance to leave the daily routines we have grown accustomed to and even fond of. Collectively, we're saddened to let go and leave behind the attachments we were forming with the people and the places. Mark announces above our nervous chatter, and sniffing noses, "OK, guys, let's load up. You've got ten minutes."

Taking long looks, we say final good-byes to our rooms, our hotel friends, and Siguatepeque, the dusty city on the Dry Canal.

The trip to Copán will be long and tiring with necessary stops for gas, snacks, bathrooms, and lunch. "Keep a tight convoy today," Mark says on the walkie-talkie. "Stay close."

We pull out.

As we head north on the future route of the Canal Seco, the highway is cluttered with construction equipment, big dump trucks, flagmen, dust, frequent stops, and short detours on graveled, cliff-hanging shoulders. Women and children on foot weave in and out of the stop-and-go traffic, trying to sell homemade snacks in plastic bags to waiting motorists. Mark says these interesting cookie-shaped wafers taste like "tree bark." No one in our group is brave enough to try any—not now. I'm thinking that most have learned their lesson, and I notice some still aren't back to normal. No more "native" snacks for them, I bet, at least not today.

Within the first hour we crest a high mountain pass, and at a walkie-talkie command, the whole five-vehicle parade pulls across on-coming traffic and into a large truck stop. We're still on the busy Canal Seco, as it's the main corridor north. Most of our vehicles line up at various fuel pumps as doors open and shoes and legs appear. Glad for a chance to get out of our cramped spaces, we waste no time in finding snacks, using bathrooms, and yakking with those from other vehicles.

In a few minutes I notice a serious powwow going on. Standing next to a fuel pump are Mark, Mike, Israel, Faríd, and Kenny. Several other men from our group shuffle closer and look on. Evidently, someone put gasoline into one of the trucks. Problem is, it's a diesel. A group of curious Honduran men gather nearby as well, surmising the problem with quizzical and even sympathetic expressions. The first issue to be settled seems to be how the mistake happened. Eyes turn to Mike, who is now putting the nozzle gingerly back in the pump.

"The handle on diesel is always green," he explains defensively. "I went for the green handle, see?" All the guys look at the handle. Sure enough, it's green.

"But here on the pump it says 'gasolina,'" Mark says, laughing. "OK, Mario, how much did you put in?"

"About fifteen gallons before Kenny stopped me."

"Well, I guess we'll just have to siphon out the whole tank." Mark says. He takes off his hat, checks his watch, and scratches his head, now wet with sweat.

The Hondurans must have understood. They circle in closer and offer to help, asking if they could have the gasolina. They quickly find a siphon hose and some five-gallon buckets. By this time Dennis, one of the men in our group, says he has a better idea. I'm surprised to learn that he's a mechanic back home in North Carolina, that is when he's not playing the grand piano or singing solos in our church. In fact, he owns the business. Everyone in the group hovers even closer, curious and anxious to help. The power and attention now shift to Dennis, and Mark studies him closely. I see that this is Dennis' domain, and he takes charge.

We step back, giving him room to work. He opens the hood and checks underneath, quickly removing the cover to a black plastic box. The maestro clearly knows what he's doing. "I need a paperclip. Steve, you got one?" he asks me authoritatively.

"Yes, sir. I'll go get it."

"Who has a pocket knife?"

"Israel does."

"Screwdriver?"

"Here."

"Hose?"

"Aquí, señor."

"Thanks, amigo. OK, now, guys, get those buckets ready. Mike, when I tell you, turn on the ignition but don't start the engine, whatever you do." Like a surgeon performing a heart transplant, he barks out orders, and the "nurses" dutifully comply. I expect to hear him shout, "Scalpel—sponge—sutures!" Mike squeezes behind the wheel and does as he's ordered. Tension builds. Mark bites his lip. The Hondurans watch his every move.

In no time Dennis connects the green siphon hose to the fuel pump and with Israel's pocket knife he short-circuits a switch in the black box. The Hondurans watch. We watch. No one breathes. Thankfully, no one lights a match.

"OK, Mike," he commands. "Turn the switch but don't crank."

In seconds we hear …. *whirr—hummm*. The fuel pump is energized and sure enough—*bzzzz—goosh*—a yellowish liquid starts flowing, squirting, and splashing. It's flowing from the green hose into the white buckets, and soon it's a solid stream.

The Hondurans smile and look at each other. Our group is amazed. So am I. "Yahoo!" someone shouts from inside the truck.

"What a great idea!" I add.

In just a few minutes the buckets are full, and the truck's fuel tank is drained. To be safe, Dennis insists that we pump in a few gallons of diesel, then pump that out too. Another powwow. Dennis wins. Problem solved.

I'm so proud of him and so impressed that we have such capable people in our group. And proud, too, that he asked *me* to find the paperclip—which I had. I'm serious—*my* paperclip. OK, I must confess that he didn't use it. He used Israel's knife instead, but I felt pretty important there for a minute and so did my paperclip—a possible moment of glory in its otherwise lowly life and a trophy I would have surely hung on my office wall back home. Nevertheless, I feel that our team could overcome any obstacle we might encounter. If the Contras or Sandinistas were to capture our capable, resourceful group, they would surely have their hands full. Dog the Bounty Hunter, Chuck Norris, and my friend, Larry, may not be needed after all.

But, you know, whether it's the Contras, Sandinistas, or simply banditos, the idea of capture is not too far-fetched. Copán is near the border of Guatemala, a country with a violent past. Only recently has Guatemala come out of the longest civil war in Latin American history (1960–1996), in which over two hundred thousand people, mostly poor civilians and indigenous indians, were killed. It was a thirty-six-year-long genocide that included over four hundred separate massacres.

In Mexico, whose border is less than one hundred fifty miles from Honduras, over five thousand murders were committed in 2008 as the result of drug cartel warfare, which was an increase of 117 percent from the year before. It appears that the situation is getting worse, especially along the USA-Mexico border. And of course we know many cases of missionaries giving their lives for the spread of the gospel. Remarkable among these stories was the murder of five young missionaries—Jim

Elliot, Ed McCully, Roger Youderian, Pete Fleming, and their pilot, Nate Saint. The Auca Indians of Ecuador killed them in 1956.

While Mark was on a mission trip to Russia once, a burglar made the mistake of breaking into his room while he was sleeping. Mark pounced on him like a bobcat on a rabbit. The intruder was trying to leave with Mark's new Minolta camera, but Mark informed him that he was *not* leaving with *his* camera. The burglar resisted but eventually left without the camera—limping. Remember, Mark wrestled in high school and is a building contractor by trade.

"Since Jacob wrestled with God, I figured it was OK if I wrestled with a Russian," Mark said with his trademark chuckle.

"Did you witness to him?" I asked, teasing.

"No, he didn't stick around long enough, or I would have."

Soon we're pulling out onto the highway once again after being sure to refuel, topping off the tank with diesel, of course, regardless of the pump handle's color.

To break the boredom in the van, one of my previous hotel roommates, a high school English teacher, suggests that I read aloud from a book I brought along. It's Patrick F. McManus's hilarious short story collection *The Bear in the Attic.* I already shared a couple of chapters with the guys in our room a few nights before; they had become curious when they heard me laughing.

When our boys were little, my wife read many of McManus's books to us on our family vacations. His books were great fun and kept us entertained and the boys distracted on otherwise long and boring road trips.

Sometime later, my reading is interrupted when we pull over for another break at a roadside filling station. (Have you noticed, or is it just me? Everything here seems to be "roadside.") Again we head for the drinks, snacks, and restrooms. For some of the vehicles, it's time for refueling again—carefully.

With our large crowd, I realize that it will be a while before I get waited on for a snack or before the only men's restroom will be available. I look around for an alternative and see a little store, a *tienda,* across a muddy side street. I hop across a small, murky ditch and enter the open-air café, approaching the counter.

An older señora is working at the grill, but an attractive, young señorita, probably her daughter, waits on me. I politely ask for a soft drink and a bag of potato chips. While the señorita is getting the items, I ask in a lowered voice the older woman who has turned to face me, "Señora, perdóname. ¿Tiene un baño?" (Excuse me ma'am. Do you have a bathroom?)

She smiles and asks, "¿Para pee-pee?"

Oh my. I've never had this response before. (May I skip the translation?)

"Sí," I reply routinely and softly in as normal a voice as possible—at least glad it was her that was asking and not her daughter.

"Ahh, sí," she says pleasantly. "Allí, afuera" (Oh, yes. Over there, outside). She points to the back of the restaurant and smiles.

Leaving my drink and chips on the counter, I slip outside nonchalantly and find a partially covered latrine—no walls, no door, just a simple trough made of blue and white ceramic tile—at least that's attractive—with a drain. Well, this is no time for modesty, I realize, as our group across the street seems to be getting ready to depart. I just hope no one is looking toward the *tienda* or toward me.

Finished, I step back into the café and find a little table bearing a basin of used soapy water for hand washing and a towel. After paying the smiling señorita for my snack, I grab it, saunter back to the filling station, and hop into the waiting van, much relieved in more ways than one. Time to break out my little bottle of hand sanitizer. See, I told you it would come in handy.

Still on the road to Copán a couple of hours later, we're searching for a place to eat. We're in the city of Santa Bárbara, and the streets are narrow, busy, and crowded. The caravan is having trouble staying in formation—too much traffic and too many *una via* (one-way) streets.

"Mark, haven't we passed this cathedral already?" I ask. It's a white Catholic church with two prominent steeples. A few minutes later I dare repeat—"Hey, Mark, we're going by that church again." (I promise, I have totally forgotten about him leaving me behind at the Texaco station.)

I'm enjoying the sights, no kidding, but Mark must be getting frustrated. I bet we pass that church three more times but I decide not to push my luck and make no further comments. Suddenly, the caravan stops at a potential restaurant. Kenny hops out for closer examination only to discover that the establishment is not a restaurant at all but a bank. *Maybe it's a mirage*, I think to myself, *a delusion before we die of starvation*. Mark gives a directive over the walkie-talkie, and apparently giving up, we head back to the highway, still not finding a place to eat. I think about the beef jerky and peanut butter crackers stashed away in my backpack, which is out of reach. On second thought, I'm afraid a food riot might erupt in the van; plus, we don't have any *boletos* to pass out.

STEVE'S SURVIVAL TIP #6: LEARN ABOUT WATER

The human body requires about two quarts of liquid per day from food or drink. In warm climates, the requirement may increase to six quarts per day.[34] But finding pure water in various parts of the world may not be easy and requires caution and good judgment.

Scientists say that during your travels the most dangerous animals you will likely encounter are swimming in the drinking water. It would be wise to remember the old saying: "Boil it, cook it, peel it, or forget it." According to a study by the World Health Organization, contaminated water accounts for 80 percent of all diseases contracted during travel and will usually affect one out of every two overseas travelers.[35] Oral and patch-type vaccines against diarrhea are still new, being tested and may not be available in the United States, so prevention is the best defense. Most overcome this disorder within forty-eight hours, but they often require medical treatment upon returning home. Five million people die annually as the result of inadequate water supply. Children are the

---

most sensitive to impure water with more than 4,000 dying per day from diseases caused by unsafe drinking water.[36]

The primary source of pathogenic contamination in drinking water, such as bacteria, viruses, and protozoa, is from human and animal excrements that have entered the water supply by various means. These germs enter our body by drinking, washing, eating, or putting contaminated hands to our faces. Though less obvious to the traveler, other contaminants, such as heavy metals and agricultural agents, such as DDT, can be found in the water supply, too.

Bacteria are single-celled organisms that reproduce rapidly in warm environments, especially in water, depending on available nutrients. Bacteria can divide in less than ten minutes. Once in drinking water, they become dangerous. The water must then be boiled, filtered, or sanitized with chemicals.

Viruses are minute parasites that bring bad effects. Since they have no metabolism of their own, they reproduce only within living cells. Because of their tiny size, they are difficult to filter; however, viruses are sensitive to heat and chemical disinfectants. Because of viruses, chemically treating filtered water is also a good idea.

Protozoans, also small but stubborn, are more highly developed than bacteria and larger, which make them easy to filter. Until they find a host, they envelope themselves in a membrane or "cyst" that is highly resistant to environmental influences. To penetrate these cysts with chemicals, an extended time period of up to four hours is recommended.

Boiling water is one of the oldest and most effective methods for sterilizing water, but it will only kill microorganisms; it won't remove turbidity or chemicals. At sea level, where water boils at 100° centigrade, water should be boiled for at least five minutes. The higher the elevation, the longer you should boil water. At twelve hundred feet, for example, water boils at 86° centigrade and should be boiled for twenty minutes.

Bottled water, generally your best bet, is not guaranteed to be germfree in every country. *Never* drink tap water or water from public fountains in tropical and subtropical countries, even in fancy resort hotels.

Surface water exposure should be met with caution. All streams, lakes, and rivers contain various bacteria, viruses, and protozoa. They may also contain dangerous parasites. In some countries fresh water may be infected with schistosomiasis, also known as "bilharzia" or "snail fever," a fluke-type worm that causes chronic illness and can damage internal organs. In children it can impair growth and cognitive development. Very serious though rarely fatal, schistosomiasis is the second-most-common parasitic disease next to malaria. It enters through the skin of the host. (Now do you understand why I avoided swimming at the waterfall?)

Chlorine bleach (sodium hypochlorite) may be used to purify drinking water of most pathogens. For the normal six percent-concentrate chlorine, use a couple of drops per quart. It's a good idea to let the water stand for a few hours to take effect on the hardest-to-kill pathogens, the cysts.

Bleach does not have the shelf life of purification tablets, so don't let your mixture get more than a few weeks old because it will lose its effectiveness.

Water purification tablets and powder offer an effective way to purify water. A recent product, developed by Procter & Gamble, is the PUR Purifier of Water,[37] which has been heralded as one of the top innovations of 2008. It claims to be "a water-treatment plant in a powder packet." The two Procter & Gamble inventors of this product won the 2006 IPOEF "Inventor of the Year Award." It's an excellent choice for large parties who need to treat water for drinking, even dirty water that could quickly clog the pores of traditional water filters. For about $15 ($11 from Wal-Mart) the box comes with six packets that treat two and a half gallons. Using a flocculent (ferrous sulfate) for sediments and a disinfectant (0.542 percent calcium hypochlorite) in sachet form, the purifier makes water ready to drink in about twenty minutes. This product has an ingredient that settles out the sediment. The treated water is then poured through a provided cloth filter before drinking. The product, which has a shelf life of three years, kills viruses and bacteria and removes dirt, cysts, and pollutants. It has been used around the world for various purposes, including disaster relief.

Another product, selling for about $10 is Potable Aqua (Wisconsin Pharmacal Company, Jackson, WI) containing twenty chlorine dioxide water purification tablets. Each tablet treats one quart of water, which is ready to drink in four hours. The active ingredients are sodium chlorite (6.4 percent) and sodium dichloroisocyanurate dihydrate (1 percent). Katadyn also makes water Micropur MP1 purification tablets.

Each of these products claims to kill or remove bacteria, viruses, and cysts, including cryptosporidium. Check with a quality outdoor sporting goods store for these and other water filtration and purification products.

Vinegar is not applicable for purifying water, but I do want to mention its versatile properties, including being a natural disinfectant that is safe to use on foods and vegetables, for example. Vinegar is a mild acid with a low pH. Some claim that normal 5 percent, white, distilled vinegar solution can kill 80 percent of bacteria and viruses. Vinegar offers a myriad of practical uses that could come in handy to the traveler, including first aid and medical purposes. It is also easy to obtain in Third World countries. Check out http://www.vingeartips.com for 1001 practical uses for vinegar.

Chapter 16

Danger—Earthquake Zone

DAY 7 CONTINUED: STILL IN THE VAN (FRIDAY)

Three-wheeled taxi

FINALLY FINDING A place to eat, we pull over and enjoy lunch at a crowded cafeteria not far from the Guatemalan border. The highway is muddy now from a light rain. I notice several colorful, little three-wheeled taxis zipping about in the busy traffic. These little motor scooters are hooded with red canvas awnings to shelter passengers. They seem to be a pretty popular and economical way to get around in this area. *Maybe they'll catch on in the States one day,* I think. The Smart Car is getting close!

Inside the cafeteria, I see no other tourists and wonder about the sanitation. I've made it for seven days now with no stomach problems, and I want to keep it that way. Considering the large number of local customers and guessing Mark has been here before, I step into the long line and take the plunge, though I'm one of the last to do so. I try to stick to cooked items—rice, beans, sautéed beef. One in our group asks me to order some "flan" for him. My Cuban-born grandmother, the missionary, made exquisite flan—a baked custard made with caramelized sauce—though as a child, I wasn't crazy about it. Ordering is easy enough: flan is *flan* in Spanish—a perfect cognate. Would that more words were this easy.

Most of us eat at the same long table and enjoy the meal as though it were our last. The food is good with generous portions, and the conversation is jovial. The meal puts us all in better spirits especially since we've been snatched from the jaws of starvation. On the other hand, this could be our last meal for a few days, if you know what I mean. *Well, if we go down,* I'm thinking, *we'll probably all go down together, "suffering for the Lord."* Nevertheless, I'm glad I still have a few stomach pills left . . . just in case. I'm not sure I'm ready to be a martyr just yet, at least not this way.

Back on the road we're finally approaching Copán, the area of the Mayan ruins we'll visit tomorrow morning. We pass through some small towns, and the topography changes dramatically. The rain begins falling more heavily.

"Tighten up the convoy, everybody," Mark says into his walkie-talkie. "Keep close." Kenny is now driving to give Mark a break. I'm keeping score on him, too. His skill level is about the same as Mark's, I decide, using my stateside grading method. I do, however, factor in the Honduran conversion scale, extrapolate the road conditions, multiply the denominator by the traffic algorithm, carry the one, and divide by the exponent of the language barrier. I even do all this in my head. Just for the record, they are both excellent drivers. I'm still alive, after all, and they get extra credit for that.

"OK, Kenny. That's minus three points already!" I say from my seat behind him.

I must confess, this ride gives me a feeling I can only describe as "masculine"—the diesel engine gunning, the van swinging us around curves like a thrown lasso, the convoy speeding on its way in close-combat formation. The trucks maneuver like fighter jets, swerving suddenly, passing or dodging deep craters in the unmarked pavement, each following in the slipstream of the other. This trip is not for sissies, the faint at heart, or the unadventurous. Someone in the back seat asks for a Dramamine.

"That's four," I call out to Kenny from my seat behind. He pulled in just a millisecond before a head-on collision with a semi hauling giant boulders. "You passed that truck so close, I could read the time on the driver's watch."

"What time did it say?" he asks calmly.

"It said it was not time to die, but we're getting close!"

Our next close call is a cement truck in our lane coming right for us. Kenny hits the shoulder just in time, then looks at me in his rearview mirror and says, laughing, "Hey, Steve, I should get a point back for that one!"

"Yeah, you're right, Kenny. And thanks. You're down to minus three again," I say, then go back to breathing. By this time they've found out about my stint as a driver's education teacher and have submitted to my qualifications to critique their driving and to give out grades. On

157

the walkie-talkie Kenny proudly announces his current grade to the other drivers in the convoy. I bet they're envious that they don't have a driver's ed teacher in their vehicle. In fact, I bet that's what they're talking about now.

Going up the mountain, I know this is an adventure. Rain comes down as we go up. The mountains get steeper, the craters deeper, and the mud muddier. I fully expect to see King Kong come traipsing out of the jungle at any minute with vines streaming down his hairy, humped back, a damsel in distress in his grip. *Who in our group might that be?* I wonder.

Entering a town, we see a large, prominently displayed sign by the roadside. *Perhaps it's a welcome sign posted by the chamber of commerce*, I think until I read it. *"PELEGRO—ZONA DE TUMULOS."*

"Hey, Steve, what does that sign say?" someone asks.

"You don't want to know."

"Yes I do. Tell me," she demands.

"It says 'Danger—Earthquake Zone.'"

"Oh, that's comforting! Thanks a lot, Steve!"

OK, now I know who'll be in King Kong's grip.

But speaking of earthquakes, a few months after our return to the States, on May 28, 2009, Honduras suffered a deadly earthquake measuring 7.1 magnitude that killed at least seven people, caused massive damage, and sent panicked people into the streets. A national emergency was declared. Since then and more recently over 217,000 people in Haiti were killed from a devastating 7.0 magnitude earthquake which occurred January 12, 2010, and another even stronger quake hit Chili, February 27, 2010, with a magnitude of 8.8, the seventh largest in history, killing hundreds.

I recall the passage in Matthew 24 where Jesus said a sign of his coming and the end of the age would be earthquakes in various places. This area near Copán and the Guatemalan border is certainly a "various place" and when they have to go to the expense to put up signs about earthquakes, it must be pretty serious. I learned that much in west

Texas where they have signs at roadside picnic tables saying, "Beware of poisonous snakes." The signs aren't there for looks, partners, they mean it. I shot two four-foot diamond-backs near my campsite which proved it to me.

Passing more road construction, barricades, wide semis, and narrow lanes, I know this is my kind of fun—adventure mixed with danger, new surroundings, challenging conditions, unfamiliar people, foreign languages, strange sights, breathtaking vistas, and heart-stopping experiences. It's a time when, seeing the poverty and living conditions of others, one doesn't dare criticize or complain. But even if we do, we'll likely hear Mark say, "¡No quejarse!" (No whining!)

At long last, Kenny turns right toward our hotel. We're checked in by armed guards and pass through a security gate to the parking lot. The hotel is open, spacious, tropical, and quite luxurious by any standards. There are two swimming pools, and exotic birds fly around the central courtyard. Coming from where we've been and what we've seen, this place is a welcome though somewhat strange culture shock. Are we still in Honduras? Is this still planet Earth? I look out the back window of my room at the lush foliage, hanging orchids, and palms. I don't see any guerilla fighters sneaking about, fortunately, but I can imagine them. If they come, we'll be like ripe plums for the picking. The only thing I could use as a weapon, a club perhaps, is Larry's water filter. The pump is cylindrically-shaped and made of steel. But don't tell this to the TSA folks, whatever you do. But next time, I think I'll put it in my checked luggage just in case someone rats on me; it will be a lot less hassle, too.

Actually, a resort like this was attacked in St. Croix, US Virgin Islands, in 1972. Eight people were killed, including a couple from Miami. The five robbers were eventually apprehended and sentenced to life in prison, but one escaped and is still at large, possibly living in Cuba.

Just before dark, we drive to the city of Copán and eat at Llama del Bosque Restaurante. There we enjoy a great meal of avocado, barbecue beef, and pork. In addition, we sample a variety of other native foods and fruits Mark and Israel recommended, such as *chorizos, guanabana,* and *maracuyá.* The serving bowls empty quickly. Afterward, though most shops are closed at this late hour, we spend some time walking about the mostly deserted town square and side streets in Copán. We feel as safe as we would have felt in our hometowns back in the States.

Returning to our hotel, Mark announces that we should assemble for an evening devotional, our last, and that Israel will give his testimony. I don't want to miss it even though it's about 9:30 P.M. Admittedly, we're all anxious for a hot shower and bed. It's been a long, tiring, and somewhat nerve-racking day, wouldn't you agree?

A short break in our hotel rooms is enough to rejuvenate us. Soon our group converges in the hotel lobby and we are directed by the concierge to a quiet area where Israel will present his testimony. Fortunately, I have my notepad and pen.

Chapter 17

Israel's Testimony

DAY 7 CONTINUED: AT THE HOTEL IN COPÁN (FRIDAY NIGHT)

TAKING MY SEAT with the rest of the group in one of the hotel's meeting rooms, Israel begins. Beth translates once more, sitting at his side.

"When I was living in Nicaragua, I realized I was not what I ought to be. I was in church. Behind the pulpit the founders' chairs were there, including my great-grandfather's chair. He was 104 years of age, I was 13, and the year was 1973. My whole family and ancestors went to that church, a beautiful, historic Baptist church. I had been part of every church program imaginable: vacation Bible school, Sunday school, everything. My dad was the preacher, and I used to go to poor villages with him, and he would conduct services at night.

"A neighbor invited me to a revival at his church. It was a tiny hut with earthen floor and wooden benches to sit on. He said they gave a book to anyone who went, and this got my attention. He said it was a book about the gospel of John. The revival lasted all week, so I went one night just to get the free book. I went, but I was uncomfortable; the benches were hard, the light dim. The preacher said regardless of your family's faith in God, if Jesus is not in your own heart, it does not count for anything. I felt he was preaching straight at me. At the invitation to accept Christ, I raised my hand from the second row. The preacher seemed to look past me but not at me. The pastor seemed not to see me. He did not say, 'God bless you' like he did for the others who raised their hand. He seemed to be ignoring me and my decision. When he gave the altar call, I went right down there to the altar. Then he looked at me and said, 'It's got to be serious, Israel, and for the Lord forever.'

"'Yes. Yes, I do,' I said, and I meant it. That was September 28, 1973, in a city in the middle of Nicaragua, the day I accepted the Lord as my personal Savior. That was about nine months after a big earthquake in our capital, Managua, which occurred beneath the center of the city, killing five thousand and leaving one-quarter of a million homeless.

"A month later we moved to Honduras. It was October 1973. Back then I didn't understand why we had to move, but we were escaping the revolution. In those days there was a civil war raging in Nicaragua. The Sandinistas were fighting against the Somoza regime. The Contras were fighting against the Sandinistas, and there was fighting even among the Sandinistas themselves. The Somozas were a family dynasty that had been in power since 1939. Daniel Ortega, who is the current president of Nicaragua, was the leader of the Sandinistas then. Thousands of people were killed in all this revolution. All my friends and neighbors were killed—every boy my age was killed. But I was in Honduras and alive.

"Five years later, I was in church preaching. I was only eighteen. I was also in seminary. God saved me from death to preach life—eternal life.

"I moved to San Pedro Sula, Honduras. I would ride my motorcycle around to preach. I learned at an early age it's not enough to be in church and say you are a Christian. Our actions speak louder than words.

"My aunt died on April 27, 2000, and my dad died the next day. It was an eleven-hour trip from San Pedro Sula to Managua, Nicaragua. Dad had colon cancer and was taking chemotherapy. The doctor gave a medicine that damaged his liver. Then a doctor from Hendersonville,

North Carolina, came to Honduras and said the medicines were killing my dad. I wanted to say to my dad's doctor, 'If my dad dies, you will die, too.'

"That very day my aunt died, but no one wanted to tell my dad because he was so sick. The next day, however, he seemed fine and could go home! We decided to go to Nicaragua for the funeral out of respect for my dad and his sister, then planned to return to Honduras.

"Friends in Nicaragua fixed up the border-crossing papers, but when we arrived, the border was closed because of the boss's birthday. I returned to a hotel at 9:00 P.M. and called my wife, Floripe. She said my dad was tired but doing fine. However, during the night, she had to take him to the hospital. About 2:24 A.M., I awoke hearing a very loud and clear voice that seemed to say, 'It is necessary that your dad's soul come to me because his body is deteriorated; your dad's soul must separate from his body because he needs to come to me.' My cousin was sleeping in the next bed. Disregarding the time, I called Floripe and asked, 'Hey Floripe, what's going on?'

"She said, 'Be strong. Your dad is dying.' But I had peace—a peace I can't describe.

"You see, if I had crossed over the border, I couldn't have called. A couple of minutes later, I called again. My dad had died. Something happened, but Floripe didn't understand. I had an unbelievable peace and … joy, joy in the Lord.

"The next day we got into Nicaragua and buried my aunt. Then the same day we made it back to San Pedro Sula to see my dad's body. It is terrible to stand in front of the dead body of one you love, but I know my dad is with the Lord. That experience helps me to this day with others going through the same thing.

"You will be glad to know, also, I didn't harm the doctor, sue him, or anything because I had this peace from God. There was comfort for my family—peace and joy. None of the words from your friends help you, but it was a help to know his soul is in the Lord's hands and it is still a comfort to me.

163

"You must be born spiritually—born again before you can grow spiritually. It is by the fruit of the spirit, not of the flesh, that we should live. We are bought with the blood from the body of Jesus Christ. Amen. That's the end of my testimony."

Then Israel opens his Bible for his finishing remarks. "Now my friends, you didn't come to help me or the people to whom you gave the boxes. Really, you have come to glorify God and to suffer for Jesus.

"Paul said in Colossians 3:17, 'And whatever you do, whether in word or deed, do it all in the name of the Lord Jesus, giving thanks to God the Father through him.' It is wonderful to meet people who want to honor and glorify God," he says.

Closing his Bible, Israel begins to smile. "Mark, Kenny, and I—well, we do some weird stuff here in Honduras. Some things are funny to us. Kids get an apple and a plate of fruit. They don't know what to do with the apple; they've heard about them but have never really seen one. They don't know how to eat it. They know about the garden of Eden, too, and are reluctant to bite! I guess that's good, yes? But we show them how and explain the difference."

We laugh and are very touched by Israel's testimony and his stories.

"Then there's ice cream," he says. "They want to save it, but it melts away. And parents want to examine the helium-filled balloons. We give out raw fabric, but they're confused as to what to do with it—make a hammock or use it as a blanket?

"When Hurricane Mitch occurred in 1998, eleven thousand people died, and eleven thousand more disappeared. The water systems went out. We asked the mission board in North Carolina to help. That's when Mark came. Four or five days later here came the money for water projects. That was over ten years ago. Then we started hearing about needs from all over. Doors opened, and we found opportunities to minister: houses, churches, stoves, bridges, water, food, mosquito fumigation, AIDS ministry, blankets, rice, and yes, even *cajitas de regalos* [little gift boxes]. That's why you have come to join us, to join the Christian Community in Honduras. Christians are working from all over the world to help Hondurans.

"In Luke chapter ten, we read that Jesus appointed seventy-two missionaries and sent them out, two by two, saying, 'When you enter a house, first say, "Peace to this house"' [v. 5]. He said stay in that house, eating and drinking whatever they give you—that is, become one of them and get to know their needs: if they're hungry, if they need water, if they need medicine or wheelchairs. He said, 'Heal the sick who are there and tell them, "The kingdom of God is near you"' [v. 10]. That's what we do: we do it with them and include them in the project. We come alongside them and help *them* do it.

"In Ephesians 2:8–10, Paul says, 'For it is by grace you have been saved, through faith—and this not from yourselves, it is the gift of God—not by works, so that no one can boast. For we are God's workmanship, created in Christ Jesus to do good works, which God prepared in advance for us to do.' Salvation is by grace, not by works. Why? To honor and glorify his name. God had planned it beforehand so you could honor his name. Sometimes we miss the opportunity. We are God's workmanship to do the best things to honor God's name."

When I hear Israel say all this, I know that his story could be the perfect ending to my story—the story that began with me asking why and looking for reasons to go or not go to Honduras. Every story must have an ending. Could this be it?

Looking over my notes, I'm thinking how Israel summarized this mission trip and the reason we came to Honduras better than I could ever explain: Then he adds, "Now my friends, you didn't come to help me or the people to whom you gave the boxes. Really, you have come to glorify God and to suffer for Jesus." With this final remark, we are dismissed. I linger for a few more minutes looking at my notes. Wow. Maybe I should just write, "The End" right here.

I'll think about it, but we still have another day and a half before we leave. God could have more planned, a dénouement perhaps. But I'm glad I came to hear Israel tonight. For me, the conclusion of our week in Honduras could be no better. I thank Pastor Israel Gonzalez for his wonderful testimony and head for my room.

165

Chapter 18

Tony and the Tour of Copán

DAY 8: THE RUINS AT COPÁN (SATURDAY)

Our tour guide, Anthony "Tony" Rios

FOLLOWING A GOOD hotel breakfast and lots of equally good coffee, we spend the morning touring the ruins of the Maya located a few miles down the road from our hotel. The site was used in the filming of Mel Gibson's movie Apocalypto in 2006, a drama about the beginning of the end of the Mayan civilization. Our tour guide is seventy-one-year-old Antonio "Tony" Rios, who has been conducting tours at Copán for thirty-six years; he even served in the U.S. Army. Rather famous among the tourists, he has been written up in many magazines and newspapers throughout the years, and he has met many celebrities. He claims that he can speak a smattering of one hundred languages and is listed in the Guinness Book of World Records, although I haven't checked. He boasts that he is not only the best guide in Copán but also an excellent journalist, singer, and "lover." He is also full of stories, jokes, memories, lore, and history—and he speaks excellent English.

A view of the ruins at Copán

Tony proudly explains to us that the Maya people lived from around 1000 B.C. to A.D. 1000 and were more advanced than the Incas or Aztecs. They had a writing system and a calendar. At its peak, Copán was the second-largest city in the Mayan empire with a population of about thirty-five thousand. Tony also informs us with a smile that the Mayas predicted the date of the end of the world.

"When?" Someone asks, of course.

"They said it would be December 21, 2012, and I plan to be here to see it," he says, smiling but glancing at our reactions.

"Can we have our money back if it doesn't happen?" a jokester asks.

Lots of movies have been produced about this date, including one recently released titled *2012*, staring John Cusack and Amanda Peet. The movie is billed as "an epic event about a global cataclysm that brings an end to the world and tells of the heroic struggles of the survivors."[38] It's a good thing they're coming out with the movie now while we still have time to go see it. On the other hand, I'll just wait until it's on TV or, if it happens, just watch from my vantage point in heaven with my fellow believers, if God allow it. Don't worry, I've read Revelation and know how it turns out.

The Mayan calendar had eighteen months and twenty days in a year, Tony informs us. So what happened to the Mayas? Archaeologists and sociologists say that they didn't survive because of soil depletion and population growth, but Tony says he'll address that later, with a knowing glance toward Mark.

He first shows us the ceiba tree, which was considered holy by the Mayas, and the needle-like spikes on the young trees that were used for Maya bleeding rituals. The Mayas were clearly a "blood cult," he admits. They knew about hallucinogenic mushrooms and other drugs, too.

"*Awwwk.*" A beautiful, large bird, a scarlet macaw, flies over our heads. Tony ducks.

"Honduran Air Force," Tony quips. "We call them *guacamayos*," he says, "*our national bird*," and we laugh at his agility and quick wit. Then we see some little furry animals that look like guinea pigs. I knew they

A *guacamaya*, the "Honduran Air Force" and national bird

would show up somewhere, but at least they've not been on our plates. Actually they are called "peccaries," and seem to be as harmless as they are curious. Tony called them "agutas," but the guidebook says they are called "quequeros" or "chanchos de monte" (mountain pigs). Next we inspect a chicle tree, a skinny little tree with a large long leaf, from which the Mayas made chewing gum. Then as we snap pictures, he guides us to various stone relics, idols, and images on the flat perimeter, surrounded by large pyramids and temples of stacked, rough stone. The Mayas even had a sports stadium. The etchings are of animals, human figures, symbols of war, skulls, blood, and smoke—universal symbols for sacrifice—and bats, a symbol of the underworld and also the symbol of the city.

Archaeologists have been working the site for years, but only 20 percent of it has been studied. Over four thousand mounds remain unopened. These mounds—time capsules dating back a thousand years or more—are likely to contain bodies, treasure, and archaeological "goodies," as Tony says. About a decade ago archaeologists discovered a trove of priceless treasures brought out of a mound—gold, silver, incredible jewels. But sometime during the night, the Mayan treasure was stolen. The thieves have never been caught, nor has the treasure ever been recovered. It seemed to be an inside job, Tony says, since the security guard later committed suicide, leaving a note but no names. *The plot for another good movie*, I think, and wonder if his death was really a suicide.

A temple and sacred obelisk

Tony and Mark are friends, especially now that Mark has toured Copán so many times; in fact, Mark could be a guide himself. Mark also keeps Tony straight when it comes to glossing over some of the theories about the demise of the Mayas, such as blaming it on the Conquistadors—saying that it would be a hundred years before they arrived—inner wars, disease, and "soil depletion." Mark laughs skeptically, pooh-poohing many of these as fabricated, politically correct excuses—"If the soil was depleted, all they had to do was go over the next hill. They had all of Honduras and Central America to cultivate. We're only talking thirty-five thousand people. That excuse is just plain stupid."

Mark's on track, I think. Thirty-five thousand would easily fit into a football stadium. I had already read what Mark is talking about in my Honduras guide book. It states, "The most accepted current explanation for Copán's collapse puts the blame on environmental factors and population growth."[39] Can you read the current political spin here? The author goes on to say, "It is likely Copán simply outgrew its environment."[40] Oh, brother. I agree with Mark and smell a cover up. I detect an agenda, too. They've taken an ancient story and perverted it into a modern day ruse. That's been tried with the Bible, too. All sorts of current trends in politics and the social agenda can be seen in movies, plays, and books. Perversions of the Bible's truth are taught and preached by the atheists and skeptical intelligentsia in our society, colleges and even seminaries.

Mark points instead to the genocide of babies in the Mayan culture, the occult, drugs, and decadent, self-centered living as the most likely reasons, verified by other societies who have followed the same path to collapse, destruction—even extinction.

Mark goes on to explain that the Mayas were an extremely bloody society—a cult, even— "blood filled," and had a low value of human life. They appeased the gods with human sacrifices, not only of adults, but also of babies—despite what the tour guides and brochures may say. Mark also ties in relevant Bible lessons and compares the Mayas to the Ammonites who worshipped the god Moloch and sacrificed their children to him (Lev. 18:21; 20:1–5). God strictly prohibited this practice with the penalty of death, he explains.

Then Mark compares the Mayas and the Ammonites to our own society, explaining that we are aborting millions of babies to our own gods, the gods of "freedom to choose" and "convenience." Our own society, with its government "chiefs" and Supreme Court "priests," has made this

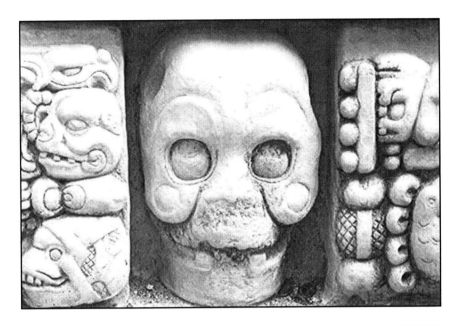

Symbols of death abound.

atrocity "legal" and defends it vehemently, and just like the Mayas, calling it a sacred "right." Yes, we're talking about killing unborn human babies. Over one million babies each year are savagely "sacrificed" so we can keep on pursuing our immoral sexual lifestyles and convenient living without children to take care of and feed. That's four thousand a day, a holocaust worse than the world has ever seen, including any war. We're not carving their tiny images on pyramids or burying their skulls in stone tombs, but we're using their body parts in the name of "research" and "science" and for other unspeakable purposes—this, too, a hot issue with the politics overshadowing the morality. Some unborn babies are even found in plastic bags in back lot Dumpsters. Are we any better than the Mayas? Will we suffer their same fate? Our nation is barely over two hundred years old; theirs was two *thousand* years old. We have advanced from the Mayas in many areas, but clearly, cannot claim moral superiority—not in this area.

An American couple tagging along with our group (for free) get mad and walk off, mumbling under their breath. I hope their parade doesn't get rained on, but they just helped illustrate Mark's point. He then points to clear evidence chiseled in stone, and Tony, when challenged with the facts, concedes. He doesn't argue against Mark's convincing proof and knowledge of the subject.

Mark also tells us, as additional evidence, that the official explanations of the Mayas' demise and their penchant for blood, death, and sacrifice have *changed* through the years, keeping pace with the "politically correct" spin of the times. Again Tony must agree with Mark. Tony not only knows this is true, but he also remembers the changing explanations. The evolution of theories can be read in some of the old brochures and books on Copán.

I'm guessing the Hondurans aren't proud of the Mayas' past, either. Perhaps mindful of the tourist dollar, they may want to gloss it over, much the way we try to gloss or skip over some of our nation's history. You would think we would want to learn from the past so mistakes won't be repeated. Tony is nevertheless eager to continue the tour. He walks us up a steep, rocky trail to the next exhibit.

As we hike, I think about how Adam and Eve tried to hide their sin. We're no different. Not only are we ashamed of sin in our own lives and try to hide it, Christian or not, we like to keep moral atrocities hush-hush, or at least put a nice-sounding term, a cutesy name or a politically correct spin on it, don't we? You know what I'm talking about. And just like the American couple, we storm away from the truth in a huff. Jesus saw this problem, too, when he walked the stony trails of Israel. We're not hiding anything from God and we're not really fooling anyone, not even ourselves. Sin is sin and it's wrong.

At the tour's end, Tony bids us farewell and goes in pursuit of his next client.

After a quick stop at the small gift shop, final visits to the *baños* (restrooms), and then swimming through the swarm of more solicitations

The Hieroglyphic Stairway at Copán

of pushy tour guides, horseback excursions, and taxi drivers, we board our trusty vehicles once more and hit the road.

We're on our way back to where we started eight days ago, San Pedro Sula, a hundred miles away, where we'll spend our last night in Honduras. Tomorrow, after doing the tourist thing at the market, we'll head to the airport for our trip home.

After a couple more hours in the van, we finally arrive at the big city of San Pedro Sula and pull though the gates to our hotel. After a lengthy wait in the office lobby and some confusion, we finally get checked in, keeping our same roommate arrangement.

The hotel is more like a big apartment complex with rows of two-story buildings and outside staircases; in fact, our rooms are really two-bedroom apartment efficiencies with a living room, kitchen, and small bath.

The maid checks the rooms and kitchen, then makes me sign an inventory list just to be sure that the items will be there when we leave. I ask for an extra blank form. I do this because it has some great vocabulary words in Spanish I can review and study later—words like *toalla* (towel), *plancha* (plate), *taza* (cup), *cuchara* (spoon), and *tenedor* (fork). Missing from the list is *jabon* (soap) and *champú* (shampoo)—I'm glad I brought my own. We'll be here for only one quick night though, so we won't really get to enjoy these comforts for long.

After quickly using our thirty minutes to freshen up, we pile back into the trucks to head out to the big mall in downtown San Pedro Sula, the second largest city in Honduras.

We pull into the covered, multistoried, concrete parking deck, and I'm already beginning to feel like I'm back in the States. The mall is really no different from some of our bigger ones. It has about four levels.

One in our group starts to weep, telling me she's thinking about our friends back in the villages. She knows that few if any of the mountain people have ever seen the inside of a place like this or the merchandise—the Rolex watches, the Gucci bags, the Florsheim and Nike shoes, golden gowns, jewels, leather coats, restaurants, gift shops, kiosks, and ATMs. It's a culture shock to us, too—and dazzling. But it's a stark and worrisome reminder about the huge chasm and the extreme differences existing in the Honduran society between the rich and poor. It's a potential source of discontent, rebellion, political opportunism, and Machiavellianism.

Nevertheless, I feel like we have changed planets and returned to a distant, yet vaguely familiar, place. Is this better? Although I'm not moved to tears, I am overwhelmed from the sensory overload—the sounds, the smells, the wealth. I see others in our group also walking around in a daze, a stupor of stimulation, dumfounded by the contrast, the un-necessity. *It awaits me back home*, I think, *for better or for worse—tomorrow.*

We assemble at a predetermined time and place in the mall for supper. It's some type of modern-styled restaurant franchise on the ground floor, where we have more confidence about the sanitation of the food and the cleanliness of the utensils. We eat a good meal and can even use our credit cards to pay.

Afterward, I make a quick stop at the ATM for a refill of lempiras, enough to last another day and finance some last-minute shopping in the morning. I insert my plastic card, and just like in the States, it asks for my preferred language, then my personal identification number, and then . . . presto! In seconds the machine spits out ready cash and a receipt. It's an amazing world.

Assembling back at our vehicles in the parking garage, it's hard to believe we're still in Honduras, a land of contrasts, a land of bright colors, blue skies, brown earth, and smiling faces.

Just before hitting the sack, my roommate and I visit the computer café downstairs at the hotel. I miss checking my e-mail regularly and reading the daily news back home, although I don't think we've missed much. Had I stayed in the States and missed this experience, I clearly see now, it would have been at my great, great loss.

Chapter 19

I Need No Other Argument

DAY 9: SAN PEDRO SULA AND HOME (SUNDAY)

THE MORNING ARRIVES too quickly, but I'm up early as usual, finding the hotel's cafeteria and coffee. I have a conversation with a Honduran waiter with shiny, combed-back hair who tells me he lived in Key West for a time and would like to go back. To get there, he says he traveled up Central America to Mexico and got across the border with the help of smugglers or *coyotes* at a cost of twenty-five hundred dollars. We swap e-mail addresses, and I tell him to let me know if he ever crosses the border again. I might consider doing it with him just for the experience. He laughs and says OK. (Don't tell this to my wife.)

Our luggage goes in the back of the pickups again, and tensions rise since we know we'll be leaving the country soon. Some of the men are investigating a minor leak spotted beneath Israel's truck. Dennis crawls underneath to see if the oil filter is leaking but soon gives his OK that it's nothing serious.

In a few minutes, as the last of our luggage is loaded and engines crank, people scramble for a seat, and for some reason I hop into Israel's truck for the ride to the market. I'm glad I did because I haven't had much one-on-one time with him and hope to learn more about him and to hear some good stories.

I'm in the front seat of his big, black, dual-wheeled, three-quarter-ton F-350 Ford with a diesel engine and, I notice, a Western hat-holder on the headliner.

"Heyyy, Mark," Israel's deep voice calls out on the toy-like walkie-talkie buried in his fist. After a click, a short blast of garbled static brings a smile to his face while, one-handed, he rotates the wheel of the "duallie." The caravan follows behind Rev. Israel Gonzalez as he twists through the parking lot and through the hotel gates and surrounding perimeter walls, but I notice only three of our vehicles are following. There should be four.

We pass a guard house and lookout tower that looks similar to a high-max penitentiary. He waves to the uniformed guards as we pass through. Looking from side to side, he pulls into the flow of traffic, slowed by a horse-drawn, rubber-wheeled wagon hauling a load of coconuts. His rearview mirror reflects the barbed wire atop the cinderblock stockade. Also disappearing from view behind us is the blue-and-pink-lettered sign—Hotel Victoria—where we slept last night. Under the shade of his floppy jungle hat, Israel focuses on the road ahead and brings the walkie-talkie back to his mouth. "OK, Mark—¡Vámonos al Mercado Guamalito—comprar Hondurano!" (OK, Mark—Let's go to the Guamalito Market to buy Honduran!)

About three or four years ago when a mission's team from Harbour Shores Church near Indianapolis, Indiana, saw the previous truck Israel was using—a dilapidated bucket of bolts—they decided to do something about it. Searching the Internet, they found this late model Ford on E-bay and bought it from a man in Louisiana—a cowboy (which explains the hat-holder). They picked it up and drove it back to Indianapolis for cleaning and servicing, then delivered it to Kenny in North Carolina who took it to the port terminal in Tampa, Florida. From there he had it container-shipped to Honduras. My head spins hearing of all they went through to get it here and I shudder thinking of all the government paperwork it must have entailed. But the truck seems well-suited for Israel and for the harsh terrain of Honduras.

I'm amazed at all that goes on behind the scenes in spreading the Gospel. I guess we don't think much about it after the offering goes into the collection plate. It's good to be reminded occasionally where our tithes and offerings go and to learn how the money is used, especially in foreign missions, where a dollar goes a long way, literally and figuratively.

Twisting our way through the back streets and through bustling intersections, I can't help but express an observation. "Israel, no one here seems to stop at the stop signs."

"Yes, they are just for decoration!" he says with a laugh.

I have also noticed, but don't mention, that there are few stoplights, and of the ones I see, most don't work. Getting through intersections seems no different to me than playing Russian roulette. I modify my question by asking, "Israel, uh…at these intersections, who has the right of way?"

"Well, all I can say is, if they're stopped, then *go*!"

"What if no one stops?"

"Well, then you have a *choque*!"

"A *choque*?"

"Yes, a crash! Except for last night, it works pretty good."

"Yeah, I heard about it. That was a close call."

Israel seems to be relaxed and in good humor, considering he was almost killed last night in a *choque* with an eighteen-wheeler. The semi didn't stop at an intersection—before or after. The pickup truck, one of the rentals in our caravan, was severely damaged in the front, but miraculously Israel wasn't hurt. Unbeknownst to us, he and Kenny spent several hours late last night at the police station and at the rental agency after the rest of us had gone to bed. I'm guessing neither one had gotten much sleep.

"But my son, Faríd, doesn't like to drive in the United States," he adds, pleasantly.

"Why?"

"He says there are too many rules!"

"Well, that semi last night wasn't following the rules, so I'm glad Faríd is behind us. Aren't you?"

"Sí, no more *choques*!"

A few minutes later, our group arrives at a large warehouse—the Mercado Guamalito—with wall-to-wall booths. Here we will shop for souvenirs before our departure from the San Pedro Sula airport. Before he turns us loose to shop, Mark says, "Inside you will see lots of souvenirs. Some are ceramic or stone replicas of the demons and gods at Copán. They were used as idols by the Mayas, and human sacrifices were made in front of them. It's your choice, but I advise you not to buy them or take them home with you—they don't represent the God we serve." I agree, and recall what the Ten Commandments has to say about this: "Thou shalt have no other gods before me"; "Thou shalt not make unto thee any graven image"; and "Thou shalt not bow down thyself to them, nor serve them" (Exodus 20:3-5). That's pretty clear, don't you think? I'll stick to my invisible God who holds the stars in place.

Again, shark-like taxis and sidewalk vendors cruise the block around the market, eying our light-skinned group as we enter, though it's true—we're not as pale as we were when we first arrived.

Mark, Israel, Faríd, Mike, and Kenny stand in the shade outside while we shop. Parked on a side street, they stay with what's left of our beleaguered vehicles, the ones they used the previous week to lug us and thousands of Christmas shoe boxes, rice, and blankets up the vaulting mountains and challenging dirt roads in central Honduras. Without these trusty chariots, we couldn't have accomplished what we did. Considering all they've been through and where we've taken them—it was sad to lose one on the "battlefield" last night—though it "died" in the line of duty. Ben Hur would have been proud.

After a couple of hours of shopping, we're back at the airport, paying our "exit tax" of about thirty-two dollars cash and checking our luggage.

I realize I have a few more minutes before I must pass through security and join the others upstairs at the Delta departure gate. Near the front door of the terminal, I offer a man my remaining lempiras for a shoeshine. He counts the bills and coins I hand him and shakes his head, telling me the money is not enough. His friends at the adjoining stands watch and laugh, but he pockets the money nevertheless and tells me to hop in the chair. I have worn the same shoes every day for the entire time—nine days—I've been in Honduras, and it's no surprise they're pretty dusty.

After brushing off the vestiges collected from the Honduran mountains and dry village roads, he rubs my brown, leather Docksiders with dark polish, then buffs them. Miraculously, it looks like my old shoes have been given a new lease on life. Truthfully, they haven't looked this good since the day I bought them. When he finishes with a few more critical strokes, a flourish, and a final inspection of his work, he asks in Spanish, "Mister, do you have a Bible?"

"Yes I do," I reply, "but it's packed in my suitcase."

"I do not have a Bible," he says. "I need a Bible."

"Next time I come, I'll bring you a Bible." I feel so bad that I don't have one handy to give him and decide to bring several next time.

"Is OK. Gracias, señor. Gracias," he says, helping me off the stand.

"¡Equalmente, mi hermano y gracias usted!" (Equally, my brother and thank you!) I tell him. Then I ask with a smile, "¿La Biblia, qué traducción, Ingles, Español o Hebreo?" (The Bible, what translation, English, Spanish or Hebrew?)

"¡Español!" (Spanish!)

"¡Esta bien!" (Very good!) We both laugh, and I turn for the escalator, admonishing myself for not being better prepared. Then I think about all the extra Bibles we have stateside, lying around unread and gathering dust.

A few hours later, buckled in a window seat and reclining once again in the cool comfort of a Boeing 737, I'm joined by two others in matching blue T-shirts—a nice-looking, middle-aged woman; and a dignified-looking gentleman about my age—uh, that would be about sixty-three. Soon we begin talking. He's a dentist from Winston-Salem, North Carolina, and she's his daughter and a nurse.

183

"Where're you from?" he asks.

Soon we discover that we actually know each other, though it's been close to fifty years. We were actually high school classmates and I remember he was an excellent and a serious student. Bruce and his daughter are returning from a mission trip in Honduras as well, but this was not their first. I ask Bruce to tell his twin brother, Lee, who was in my Latin class and who became a banker, "hello" for me and to thank him for giving me my first loan. The event was back in the sixties when I was a school teacher (in my twenties) living in Puerto Rico. I used the money to buy my first sailboat, a twenty-seven foot fiberglass sloop. It had been a great investment and a source of many wonderful adventures. Nevertheless, it makes me feel good to be in Bruce's fine company once again, knowing that we shared similar experiences and the same . . . well, the same reason for going to Honduras.

The jet is racing north. I'm looking down once again on the flat Caribbean shimmering in sapphire blue and emerald green. We're skirting the coral reefs of Belize and the Yucatán Peninsula, this time to our left, still climbing at twenty-nine thousand feet and going five hundred fifty miles per hour. I watch our flight path on the seatback monitor. Honduras is fading fast behind. Nothing to do now but to sit quietly, listen to the stream of air over the fuselage, and think.

How did this all start?

I think back to the night at the restaurant in North Carolina—the colorful photographs that were so persuasive, the close-ups and earth tones that appealed to me, the dirt roads, the mud huts. I recall the gleaming smiles on tender faces and the wide eyes of barefoot children who needed no translation. I recall pictures of the vistas of verdant greens—trees, mountains, sleepy hillside farms—and distant hues of watery blue and misty clouds—all the reasons that had gone into my "yes box." Now those pictures have come to life. They're no longer pictures but memories.

Then I think of all the things I've seen and done this past week. I can still see the images in my mind and hear the voices and laughter. I remember the stories. I can hear the singing and wailing prayers with lifted hands. I see the children, their smiles, the boxes, and their curious wonder. I remember the wrinkles in the old lady's face and the tears in her eyes. I remember the little girl's kiss in my dream.

These are people who love their children. The family unit is honored, respected, and protected. They are willing to reach out to visitors from far-off places, to serve meals and coffee, to give hugs and hospitality, and to offer all they have—if only love. They have names, they have wants and needs. They are more than photographs; they are the children of God, and he loves each one.

Yes, I have a lot to think about and a lot to remember, too, especially the questions that pestered me at the beginning. I remember searching for reasons to go, or even one *good* reason, asking—Why do it? Why me? Why should anyone become a missionary, risking life and limb in a hostile environment to go to some far off country? It could also be asked, why should anyone walk next door to witness to a neighbor? The reasons to do so are the same, actually.

God said do it. I should have known that. You might say, the answer was staring at me all along. The answer was easily found on our T-shirts, "Go ye into all the world, and preach the gospel to every creature" (Mark 16:15), and it was my grandfather's life verse I thought I knew so well. Jesus sent his disciples out, as workers in the harvest field, two by two, saying, "Go...I send you forth as lambs among wolves" (Luke 10:3). He instructed Legion, the demon-possessed man he had healed, to go and tell his family how much the Lord had done for him and how mercy had been shown for him (Mark 5:19).

God did it himself. "He came unto his own, and his own received him not," (John 1:11) and "The Word was made flesh and dwelt among us" (John 1:14). Jesus did not stay in heaven but instead, he left his father's side and came to us (Romans 8:34).

Jesus modeled it. He went to towns and villages. He preached on the water, in the hills, in the country, and in the gardens. He brought salvation to homes and temples, to courts and palaces, to valleys and mountain tops, and down to the seashore where fishermen wash their nets. He brought his love all the way to the cross.

God loves us. He came because of his love—his love for us—and he wants us to have eternal life. "For God so loved the world, that he gave his only begotten Son, that whosoever believeth in him should not perish, but have everlasting life" (John 3:16).

I've learned a lot, and yes, I now know the answer to my question. It was given to me by the old lady and her daughter at Pimienta, the deacon Felípe at Los Llanos, and the elderly campesinos at Río Bonito. Israel confirmed it Friday night. The reason is the perfect reason and the only reason anyone should ever need. It's the reason God came to us. Why? It was because God loved and God gave. That's it.

God's reason became flesh. He is our priceless treasure and became our missionary from heaven bringing the ultimate gift—eternal life—to the world, if only we would accept and believe in him. His name is Jesus. His mission is love.

> I need no other argument,
> I need no other plea,
> It is enough that Jesus died,
> And that He died for me.

—Lidie H. Edmunds,
"My Faith Has Found a Resting Place"

A final word, amigos. Remember this—Come when God calls you, go where God sends you, do what God tells you, and grow where God plants you. May God richly bless you with his eternal treasures.

Thank God we have come out from those depths!

—Steve

Epilogue

I ARRIVED IN Charlotte late that night. I had trouble finding my car in the dark, even though I had written down the lot and row numbers. Then I couldn't find my keys—they were buried somewhere in my luggage. Fortunately, I remembered my hidden set and used them instead. Although late, my wife waited up for my arrival and insisted on seeing my photographs and hearing about the trip taken by her "reluctant missionary."

Adios y vaya con dios (Goodbye and go with God),

—SN

My Invitation to You

If you haven't done so already, won't you receive God's "gift box" of eternal life sent especially to earth for you?

Here is how you can receive Christ as your personal Savior:

1. Admit your need. (I am a sinner.)
2. Be willing to turn from your sins. (Repent.)
3. Believe that Jesus Christ died for you on the cross and rose from the grave. (Accept his sacrifice for your sins.)
4. Invite Jesus Christ by prayer to come in and control your life through the working of the Holy Spirit.
5. Accept and receive Jesus Christ and welcome him as your Lord and Savior! (Read John 3:16.)

And to further help in your Christian growth and life:

6. Find and attend a local Bible-believing, Bible-teaching church and begin your own journey of personal growth in the Christian faith.
7. Connect with some Christian friends and mentors.
8. Tell others about Jesus and find ways to serve him.

You may order additional copies of this book for your friends, church, youth, or mission groups by visiting my Website—www. JStephenNorwood.com. Thank you for reading *Confessions of a Reluctant Missionary*. I hope you have enjoyed it.

—SN

Appendix 2

Letter from C.R. Stegall (author's grandfather), 1913, in response to his sister who was trying to dissuade him from becoming a missionary.

(Reproduced verbatim. Scripture references cited for the reader's convenience.)

Georgia Students' Missionary League
Atlanta, Ga.
April 24, 1913

Dear Pauline,

I was quite glad to hear from you. It is seldom that I have that pleasure. I appreciate the fact that I am wanted in this country but that is quite out of the question. Your arguments are all good in their way but I think I can answer all of them to perfect satisfaction, and that directly from the Bible. Don't take my word, read it for yourself.

Your main objections to my going is, it seems to me are, (1) worry to our father, (2) father is old, (3) I am too young, (4) inexperienced, (5) unused to hardships.

As an answer to (1), read Matthew 10:37 [He that loveth father or mother more than me is not worthy of me: and he that loveth son or daughter more than me is not worthy of me.] (KJV)

As an answer to (2), read Luke 9:59-60 [And he said unto another, Follow me. But he said, Lord, suffer me first to go and bury my father. Jesus said unto him, Let the dead bury their dead: but go thou and preach the kingdom of God.] (KJV)

As an answer to (3), read Luke 18:29-30 [And he said unto them, "Verily I say unto you, There is no man that hath left house, or parents, or brethren, or wife, or children, for the kingdom of God's sake, who shall not receive manifold more in this present time, and in the world to come life everlasting."] (KJV)

Here on this promise lies my strength and it was spoken following his calling of the young man.

(4) Romans 5:3–4 [And not only so, but we glory in tribulations also: knowing that tribulation worketh patience; And patience, experience; and experience, hope:] (KJV)

(5) Luke 9:57 [And it came to pass, that, as they went in the way, a certain man said unto him, Lord, I will follow thee whithersoever thou goest.] (KJV)

Also read Isaiah 41:10 [Fear thou not; for I am with thee: be not dismayed; for I am thy God: I will strengthen thee; yea, I will help thee; yea, I will uphold thee with the right hand of my righteousness.] (KJV)

You say that Papa is greatly worried about it. He has not written me a word since I wrote him my plans. I would like to see you and Hershel and the rest too before I leave, for great things could happen in seven years—the length of my first stay—health permitting. It is probable that I shall sail from New York July

Letter from C.R. Stegall (author's grandfather), 1913,
in response to his sister who was trying to dissuade him from
becoming a missionary.

2nd at 1 A.M. on the *Mauretania*. Will reach my station in the
Congo some ten weeks later. Write again when you can.

Love to you both,
Carroll (C.R. Stegall, age 22)

Author's note: After my grandfather married and became a missionary to Africa, his father (Robert Blackwell Stegall of Roswell, Georgia) accepted his son's decision and became one of his strongest supporters. He was very proud of him to the day he died, April 18, 1935, at the age of 93. My mother remembers first meeting him, but could not speak English at the time.

Appendix 3

Ministry Support

IF YOU WOULD like to contribute to the Christian Community in Honduras and support the work of Mark Searcy and Israel Gonzalez, you may send your contribution to the following:

Kenny Barnwell
Christian Community in Honduras
P.O. Box 606
Fletcher, NC 28732
USA

Endnotes

Preface

1. Tshiluba belongs to the Bantu branch of the Niger-Congo languages. It is the language of the Baluba people. Tshiluba is spoken by about 6.3 million people in the Kasaï Occidental and Kasaï Oriental provinces of the Democratic Republic of the Congo.

   Of possible interest to the reader, the Bantu word identified in June 2004 by Today's Translations, a British translation company, as the most untranslatable in the world: *ilunga*, in the Tshiluba tongue, means "a person ready to forgive any abuse the first time, to tolerate it a second time, but never a third time." However, it is more likely to be a personal name rather than a difficult word. http://en.wikipedia.org/wiki/Tshiluba_language

   Author's note: My mother's African name is "Sankisha Mutchima," ("Sanky" for short) which means "To make the heart happy." Now at the age of 94, she has always lived up to her name.

Chapter 1

2. Chris Humphrey, *Moon Handbooks Honduras* (3ʳᵈ. ed.; California: Avalon Travel, 2003) p. 3.

3. "Honduras: Location, Size and Extent," Encyclopedia of the Nations, http://www.nationsencyclopedia.com.
4. "Central America and the Caribbean: Honduras," CIA World Factbook, https://www.cia.gov/library/publications/the-world-factbook.
5. "Background Note: Honduras," The World Bank, http://web.worldbank.org/WBSITE/EXTERNAL/COUNTRIES/LACEXT/HONDURASEXTN/0,,menuPK:295076~pagePK:141159~piPK:141110~theSitePK:295071,00.html.
6. "Honduras History," HONDURAS.com, http://www.honduras.com/history/.

Chapter 4

7. "Health Information for Travelers to Honduras," Centers for Disease Control and Prevention, http://wwwnc.cdc.gov/travel/destinations/Honduras.aspx.
8. "Major Infectious Diseases-Honduras," Index Mundi (2009), http://www.indexmundi.com/honduras/major_infectious_diseases.html.
9. Ibid.
10. Chris Humphrey, *Moon Handbooks Honduras* (3rd. ed.; California: Avalon Travel, 2003) p.81.
11. "The Snakes of Honduras," *Disease Vector Ecology Profile*, (Washington, D.C.: Armed Forces Pest Management Board. July, 1992), p. 35, http://www.afpmb.org/pubs/dveps/honduras.pdf.
12. Larry David Wilson and James R. McCraine, "The Conservation Status of the Herpetofauna of Honduras," Amphibian and Reptile Conservation, http://www.ncbi.nlm.nih.gov/pmc/articles/PMC289144/#arc-0000012-Wilson16 [Wilson L.D, McCranie J.R. Update on the list of reptiles known from Honduras. *Herpetological Review.* 2002; **33**(2):90–94].
13. "Arthropods of Medical Importance" (Honduras), *Disease Vector Ecology Profile* (Washington, D.C.: Armed Forces Pest Management

Board. July, 1992), p. 32, http://www.afpmb.org/pubs/dveps/honduras.pdf.

14. "Honduras History Overview," Online Guide to Honduras, http://www.honduras-information.hotelhonduras.com/Honduras-History.htm.

15. "El Salvador vs. Honduras, 1969: The 100-Hour War," Central and Latin America Database, Air Combat and Information Group, http://www.acig.org/artman/publish/article_156.shtml.

16. "Honduras History," HONDURAS.com, http://www.honduras.com/history/.

17. "Honduras," Travel and Living Abroad, http://www.fco.gov.uk/en/travel-and-living-abroad/.

18. "Ring of Fire Volcanoes," Universe Today, http://www.universetoday.com/guide-to-space/earth/ring-of-fire-volcanoes/.

19. "Lluvia de Peces," Wikipedia, http://en.wikipedia.org/wiki/Lluvia_de_Peces.

20. "Honduras: Country Specific Information," US Department of State, http://travel.state.gov/travel/cis_pa_tw/cis/cis_1135.html.

21. "Health Information for Honduras-Avoid Injuries," Centers for Disease Control and Prevention, http://wwwnc.cdc.gov/travel/destinations/honduras.aspx.

Chapter 5

22. "Malaria," Centers for Disease Control, http://www.cdc.gov/malaria/.

23. "Morbidity and Mortality Report, Surveillance Summaries," Centers for Disease Control, volume 58 (April 17, 2009), p. 11, http://www.cdc.gov/mmwr/PDF/ss/ss5802.pdf.

Chapter 6

24. Christian Community in Honduras, Lajas, Taulabé.

25. "And he said unto them, Go ye into all the world and preach the gospel to every creature. He that believeth and is baptized shall be saved." Mark 16:15-16 (KJV).

Chapter 7

26· "Honduras Clinic," Rivers of the World, http://www.row.org/countries/honduras/clinic.htm.

Chapter 8

27. The Duvaliers employed the MSVN, a "national security" militia, called the *Tonton Macoutes* (translates as "Uncle Gunnysack" originating from Haitian Creole mythology) in a reign of terror against any opponents, including those who proposed progressive social systems. Those who spoke out against Duvalier would disappear at night, or were sometimes attacked in broad daylight. They were never seen again. They were believed to have been abducted and killed by the *Tonton Macoutes* (MSVN) as a result. Anyone who challenged the MVSN risked assassination. Their unrestrained terrorism was accompanied by corruption, extortion, and personal aggrandizement among the leadership. Source: Wikipedia, http://en.wikipedia.org/wiki/Tonton_Macoute.

Note: Having sailed into Haiti myself two months after the death of "Papa Doc," Jean-Claude's father, I had heard rumors that he had a shark-pit somewhere he used for the quiet disposal of opponents. Jean-Claude was only 19 when he inherited the presidency. While there, sailing into two different ports, I kept a low-profile and didn't stray too far from my boat.

Chapter 9

28. "Port, Highway Projects Boost Honduras Logistics," Site Selection Magazine Online, World Reports, September, 2008, http://www.siteselection.com/issues/2008/sep/World-Reports/.

29. Luxner, Larry, "As Panama Plans Canal Expansion, Neighboring Countries Eye Alternatives," *Mesoamerica*, Vol 26, No. 5, (May 2007) p.3, http://www.mesoamericaonline.net/MES0_ARCHIVES/Features/FEAMAY07.pdf.

30. "Building a Dry Canal," Europa-Honduras, http://www.europa-honduras.eu/article_buildingadrycanalhondurasandelsalvadorsnew-landroutebetweentheatlanticandpacificwillcomplementthepanamac anal_170.html.

31. OK, for you film-purists, I know this is a famous misquotation. Rick (Humphrey Bogart) actually said to Sam, "You played it for her ('As Time Goes By') and you can play it for me," followed by "If she can stand it, I can! Play it!" By the way, Sam (Dooley Wilson) was a drummer in real life and could not actually play the piano. Source: Wikipedia, http://en.wikipedia.org/wiki/Casablanca_(film)#Quotations.

Chapter 11

32. "Honduras," Rivers of the World, http://www.row.org/countries/honduras/default.htm.

Chapter 13

33. Christina Mandzuk and Lynette Schrowe, "Honduras Stove Project: Phase II," (MPH Candidates, Global Health & International Medicine, Indiana University School of Medicine. July 26, 2007), http://www.medicine.iu.edu/documents/DPHDocuments/InternationalHealth/Phase%20II%20-%20AMT%20Version.pdf.

Chapter 15

34. "Drinking Water," Water Guide for Safe Driving Water. Katydyn. www.katadyn.com.

35. Ibid, p. 7.

36. "Safe Drinking Water," P&G Sciences Institute, http://www.pg.com/pghsi/safewater.

37. "Safe Drinking Water," P&G Health Sciences Institute, http://www.pg.com/pghsi/safewater/.

Chapter 18

38. "2012,"Internet Database (IMDb), http://www.imdb.com/title/
   tt1190080/.
39. Chris Humphrey, *Moon Handbooks Honduras* (3rd. ed.; California:
   Avalon Travel, 2003) p. 236.
40. Ibid.

About the Author

J. Stephen Norwood, BS, MAEd, EdS, a retired public school administrator with over thirty-three years of experience, lives in Hendersonville, North Carolina. He taught in Georgia, Puerto Rico, Florida, and North Carolina. He also held central office positions in two school systems and served as principal at several schools, including Mud Creek Baptist Christian School in Hendersonville following his retirement. He has served on the NC PTA Board of Managers, as president of the Hendersonville Lions Club, and on numerous other community organizations. He is a formerly licensed sea captain and ham radio operator.

Steve recently wrote a novel, *Ulicee's Mansion,* which is based on a true story. Steve's articles have appeared in the Indiana School Boards Association journal; *Public Telecommunications Review;* as well as *Voice*

and *Leadership*, both journals of the North Carolina School Boards Association. He wrote the video script for a nationally recognized family literacy program and assisted in the filming and story development for the award-winning documentary *The Heart of Texas*, upon which his novel is based.

His wife, Debbie, is a high school teacher, and they have two sons. John, a graduate of NCSU, is an industrial engineer and project manager living in Raleigh, North Carolina and David, a graduate of USMA, is an officer in the U.S. Army, stationed at Ft. Hood, Texas.

Visit the author's Web site at http://www.JStephenNorwood.com

To order additional copies of this book call:
1-877-421-READ (7323)
or please visit our Web site at
www.pleasantwordbooks.com

If you enjoyed this quality custom-published book,
drop by our Web site for more books and information.

www.winepressgroup.com
"Your partner in custom publishing."

LaVergne, TN USA
02 November 2010

203109LV00002B/6/P